REALITY CHECK

One Father's Opinion On World Affairs

REALITY CHECK

One Father's Opinion On World Affairs

Mike O'Byrne

Library of Congress Cataloging-in-Publication Data

O'Byrne, Mike, 1938–
Reality check : one father's opinion on world affairs / by Mike O'Byrne.
p. cm.
ISBN 0-938106-22-8
1. United States—Economic conditions—1945– 2. United States—Politics and government—1945– 3. Economic history—1945– 4. Energy industries—United States. 5. Family—Economic aspects—United States. 6. Quality of life—United States. I. Title.
HC106.5.017 1996
330.973'092—dc20 96-44112
CIP

This book is a personal essay by the author and in no way reflects the views or positions of those quoted or of those individuals or agencies whose data is incorporated here to illustrate these opinions. The opinions expressed are solely those of the author.

Book design and production by Laing Communications Inc., Redmond, Washington and Edmonton, Alberta.

For more information or to order copies, please contact Laing Communications Inc., (206) 869-6313.

Printed in Canada

To my wife, Penny, and to our children, Jennifer, Greg, and Andrew,
with fond memories of our dinner table conversations.

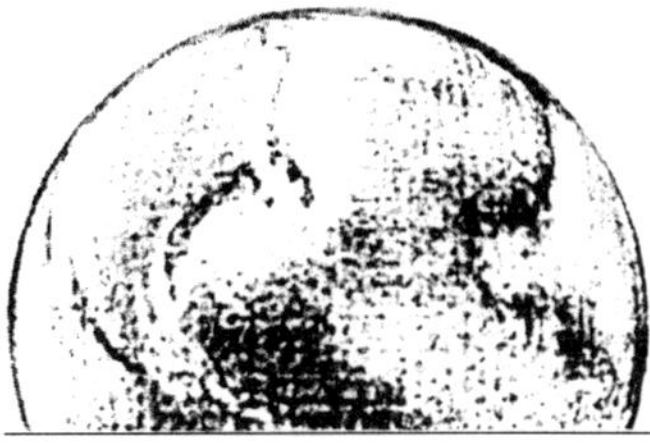

Contents

Foreword

Mike O'Byrne.

My dad.

As long as I can remember, my dad has been someone who knows his mind. He knows what is good and has been able, in almost every instance I can remember, to do the right thing at the right time. This might just be a lot of luck, but I believe he always has had the intent to follow a good path. His views on what the world should be like, what is possible to attain and what the future holds reflect this drive. As I've grown older I realized that he has one view, one perspective. I don't necessarily agree with all he believes but most of the time his viewpoints seem to hold truer than most.

As I grew older into adulthood, our family would gather for dinner on special occasions. We'd enjoy the meal and then discuss everything under the sun. Our opinions varied. My sister Jennifer was always the most liberal among us. My Mom would quietly (tongue in cheek) let us know her opinion—usually, but not always, a conservative viewpoint. My brother Andrew soaked it all in, using the information to frustrate some of his more liberal teachers. I tended to play the devil's advocate on a lot of the issues. My father, well, he tended to be the instigator in our discussions, raising the issues and letting us know clearly where he stood. We each had the opportunity to take our stances and to point out the various, obvious weak points in others' arguments. Sometimes there was agreement; a lot of the time there was not.

During one of these discussions, somebody suggested that Dad write a book on his beliefs, he being the one who led our conversations. At first I think he pondered the idea, but once it was stated it seemed the obvious thing for him to do. For more than a year, we kept saying, "You should write a book." He finally just sat down and did it.

He had never written a book before, although he had done a lot of writing.

He had never done research for a book before; however he was an avid reader of serious information.

After what seemed an impressively short time, he had his book written—fully researched with all the evidence he could gather to prove his beliefs. I was very impressed, as we all were.

He had done it again. He had led his life down the good path as he has always done, this time achieving what's said in one of the best clichés ever: "Whatever you put your mind to you can accomplish."

This book shows how a lot of things that are painted as doom-filled predictions by the press and other information providers are actually improving. The book is split into eight chapters covering topics ranging from energy to crime. In each chapter, he presents his viewpoint and supports it with strong facts. I don't agree with every point he raises and I definitely have some more questions to ask him at our next dinner, such as: Will extremely high energy prices in the future eventually force energy into scarcity? Will the growing population in the Third World cause irreparable harm to the environment, due to pollution, before it develops enough to control itself and the problem? Arguments could always arise about other factors not included, such as the growth of crime among our youth and how it affects the quality of our education. I agree with his underlying theme that energy prices will rise to supply and demand equilibrium and that a country must achieve economic maturity to effectively control its pollution. The information he gathered and used to support each of his points shows this to be the case.

The points he has expressed should be taken further by others. They show that our world is a work in progress and that nobody handed us a "how-to book" about managing our Earth. We have had to make mistakes and learn from them. My Dad's book shows that we have learned a lot and continue to learn more each day. It gives me confidence that we now know enough about our mistakes so that we will make fewer mistakes in the future. We now might be able to run our planet without damaging it. The same could be said about our country and our society. We have had to teach ourselves so much—and aren't the things we have accomplished quite remarkable!

Greg O'Byrne
October 1996

Introduction

LIFE'S PROBLEMS OFTEN CAN BE SOLVED around the dinner table, it seems. This has certainly been true for our family. My wife and I have always encouraged free discussions over our nightly meals with our children. As a result, every possible topic, ranging from daily happenings, gardening, dating, and grocery prices to politics and economics has been opined and analyzed.

In these talks over the years, and as my older children went off to college, I noticed that they increasingly seemed to echo the conventional wisdom that the world, and in particular the United States, was in trouble and that things were continually getting worse. My personal belief, and what I think the facts support, is that exactly the opposite is true.

After years of being a pontificating father and counteracting all the doom and gloom at home, I was told by my oldest son, "Dad, you should write a book." This essay is a result of that challenge.

In the early years of our discussions, it seems that we were discussing what is now called political correctness, but we didn't know it at the time. Many of our subjects were ones with which our society is still struggling today as we move into the next millennium.

My belief on all of these subjects is that the conventional wisdom or the politically correct positions are exactly backwards from reality, or the opposite of the truth. These backwards positions cause us to make many wrong decisions in our society. These decisions often make matters worse rather than better, a reality in politics that is called the law of unintended consequences.

Although our discussions around the dinner table have covered numerous topics, the ones included here seem to be the most important to our country and society. They are:

I: Energy. Most people believe that the world is running out of energy. The opposite is true. The world is actually awash in energy and will be so for the foreseeable future.

II: Transportation. Many people, including politicians, believe that we can force people out of their private cars through incentives or by inconveniences. Unfortunately, this doesn't work because most people continue to prefer to own and operate a private car. Transportation plans should reflect this reality. Attempts to force people out of their cars are based largely on our fear that we are running out of energy, and that our cars use too much energy. These fears are unfounded, as discussed in Chapter 1.

III: Pollution. We assume that pollution levels in the United States are high and are getting higher. The opposite is actually true. We should recognize that pollution is steadily being reduced. We should understand why this is happening and should continue with the policies that have given us success. As stated by Gregg Easterbrook in *A Moment on the Earth*, "In the Western world, pollution will end within our lifetimes."

IV: Population. Ever since Malthus, we have assumed that growth in population will eventually overrun the world and we will not be able to support ourselves. This hasn't happened, and, in reality, probably won't. The larger problem is despotic governments around the world, their civil wars, and their deliberate starving of their people. There simply isn't a population or food-source problem in the world's liberal democracies.

V: Education. We make the assumption that our public education system is broken. It isn't and is probably doing as good or better job than ever. For example, compare which countries win the majority of the Nobel prizes (see Figure 5-1).

VI: Crime. Crime in America is the top item on many people's "worry" list. Although it is a problem, particularly violent crime among our youth, perhaps it isn't as bad as we all think it is and, just maybe, it actually is improving.

VII: Trade balances. We assume that negative trade balances are bad. The reverse can be true and is true in the case of the United States. Our persistent negative balance of trade for the last several years has actually contributed to our prosperity and growth.

VIII. Productivity. We are constantly told that productivity in the United States is bad and is getting worse. Nothing could be further from the truth. The United States is the most productive country in the world by a wide margin and has been so for a very long time.

These eight topics are all very important to our society. We make decisions every day concerning these areas. If we are making those decisions based on false or backwards assumptions, then there's a good chance the decisions will be wrong. Even if they aren't completely wrong, they won't be as good as they would be if based on fact and not on assumptions.

My background prior to writing this book comes from a career spent largely in the energy, or energy-related, field. I began as a mechanical engineer with a nuclear engineering specialty. I majored in this field because at that time I believed that the world would soon run out of fossil fuels and that nuclear power would be the energy source for the future. With my engineering degree, I spent the first eight years in the nuclear power field in the U.S. Navy's nuclear submarine fleet.

After leaving the Navy, I joined the Kenworth Truck Company where, over the next 15+ years, I rose to the position of General Manager. Kenworth, as one might imagine, is a major user of fossil fuels and is intimately involved with the world's transportation and energy issues. In addition to making trucks for the United States, Kenworth is a major supplier of oil field trucks to the Middle East and other parts of the world. My experience at Kenworth modified my outlook on the world's energy situation and on the relation of nuclear energy to fossil fuels. While at Kenworth, I had the opportunity to attend Stanford University for a summer. Some of the economic lessons I learned there relating to the world energy situation also affected my perspective on the topics discussed in this book.

During this time, I became somewhat politically active, serving as a Councilman in my local town and serving on the boards of political action groups in the local area.

After leaving Kenworth and its parent company, PACCAR, I spent several years as an independent businessman and consultant to start-up companies. This resulted in quite a political and economic learning experience about the realities of operating a small company in the political-economic climate that we live in today.

Following my time as an independent businessman, I was President and CEO of two companies, one a software company, the other a heavy equipment distributor. While quite diverse businesses, the CEO role in these companies has caused me to become very politically active in order to try to influence political decisions in the best interests of the companies. I have now retired from the heavy equipment distributing company and am consulting in the areas of management and marketing.

I have briefly explained my background to show how my thinking has been influenced by my experiences and how it has changed over time. I think I bring a unique experience base to these issues that can be useful to others.

Early in my career, particularly from an engineering perspective, I believed that problems tended to be technical in nature and could be solved using our tremendous technical capabilities. In the energy field, specifically, I believed that as we ran out of fossil fuels, we would replace them with nuclear power. I think that many people held that belief in the '50s and '60s.

Over time, though, I have slowly changed my perspective and beliefs. As an older, and more experienced, person, I now believe that these problems tend to be more economic in nature. By "economics" I mean the old-fashioned definition of political economics. It seems that the politics of many of these issues are more important than the facts related to them.

Introduction

Historically, economics wasn't treated as an independent subject. The subject, rather, was political economics. I think that was the correct treatment. Politics and economics, particularly as they relate to the great issues of our times, can't be separated. In all of the subjects discussed in this book, the reality is that the politics, as well as the economics and facts, will strongly influence the decisions taken. If we let politics alone drive our decisions without enough technical and economic input, then we are naive. I hope that this book can help in some small way to make our society better.

You will find that this book is unabashedly pro-capitalism and pro-democracy. Liberty and the ability of free people to make the major decisions affecting their lives without undue interference from their government is a major factor in the huge successes of modern civilization. The areas of the world where people are not enjoying the fruits of our modern world are, without exception, where despotic governments oppress their own people. This, again, is a political-economic problem and will be noted several times in the book.

The eight topics that I have chosen to discuss are all very important to our lives. I think that making proper, well-considered decisions about all of them is important to our future. I hope that this book will help all of us to make better choices.

1

Energy

THE WORLD IS RUNNING OUT OF ENERGY! This has been the prevailing opinion of most people for more than twenty years. Nothing could be further from the truth. The world is awash in energy and will be for the foreseeable future. Unfortunately, we are making many decisions affecting our lives and our future based on the false assumption that energy is running out, and these decisions are often wrong and not in our best interests.

Why is this? Why is it so easy to believe that we are running out of energy and most other resources when it actually isn't true?

The answer is simple, but requires some understanding of the various factors that contribute to the perception that many of us have. These factors include physics and engineering, geology, history, economics, and a lot of global and U.S. politics.

My own understanding and growth in this area parallels in many ways what we all have gone through for the last quarter century and before. As a senior in high school in 1956, I wrote a term paper on how the world was running out of conventional energy sources and how nuclear power had to be the answer for the survival of our civilization. I believed this strongly enough to study nuclear power in college and to spend eight years in the nuclear field in the Navy after graduation.

After leaving the Navy, I joined Kenworth Truck Company as an Applications Engineer. It was my job to ensure that customers' large diesel trucks worked best for their job needs. That was in 1969, before the energy crisis of 1973. Fuel was cheap and we were working on installing bigger engines, gas turbine engines, and other improvements to move in the direction of making faster, bigger, and more productive trucks. Fuel economy was not a significant issue.

Then in 1973 everything quickly changed. Fuel availability and fuel economy suddenly became of paramount importance. Our industry went into a major recession and the whole thrust of Kenworth's engineering development changed. The gas turbine projects, as an example, were immediately scrapped because gas turbine engines could not come close to diesel engines in fuel economy.

At Kenworth, we did many things to react to what we thought was the new reality. We had long been the primary supplier of off-road oil-field trucks to the Middle East and that became a more important business for us. We started developing coal trucks because we thought that coal would surely grow in importance in the years to come. And we went to work, along with our suppliers of engines, transmissions, axles, tires, and other parts, to make our trucks more fuel efficient.

Our suppliers made major changes also. Our major engine supplier committed hundreds of millions of dollars to a whole new engine program because its forecasts had predicted that oil would increase to more than $100 per barrel by 1985.

Our country changed dramatically overnight. Suddenly, big, gas-guzzling cars were out and small, fuel-efficient cars (usually Japanese) were in. We lost confidence in ourselves when Detroit couldn't reinvent itself fast enough to meet our sudden change in demand. We all turned our thermostats down in the winter and up in the summer. We started insulating our houses better, improved our construction standards, established a national 55 mph speed limit, and waited in line at the gas pumps.

Looking back twenty-three years later, in 1996, what was really happening then? We haven't yet run out of oil. In fact, the price of it, when corrected for inflation, is below what it was in 1973 (Figure 1-1). Enormous amounts of money have been spent on development of new energy sources and much of the money has been wasted. The huge financial losses in nuclear power, oil shale development, coal, solar power, and natural gas developments are a testimony to the fact that we really aren't running out of or short of energy—or of oil.

What happened? It's time for a little history.

History of the Energy Supply

To understand the energy story, we have to go back to the years after World War II. At that time, the United States and Canada were the only developed economies that had escaped relatively unscathed from the war. The United States was facing the growth of Communism around the world, especially in Russia and China. To the everlasting credit of the United States, our policy was to try to help rebuild the countries that had been devastated by the war. Presidents Truman and Eisenhower can take great credit for this time in our history.

Many tactics were used to help this recovery and to stop the expansion of Communism. It is well known how the Marshall Plan in Europe and the enlightened administration in Japan helped both get back on their feet. We also helped to form NATO, put troops in Europe and elsewhere around the world, and fought a war in Korea during this period.

During this time, the United States was the world's largest oil producer and was also the world's largest oil exporter. We were so strong that we were able to control the price of oil and to dominate the world market.

It was at that time that the United States made a strategic decision. It was determined that it was in our best interest and in the best interest of the free world to ensure that an ample supply of cheap energy was available to power the post-war recovery and to help the western countries fend off Communism. We were, in fact, the first oil price controller prior to the Organization of Petroleum Exporting Countries (OPEC). However, our goal was to keep the price of energy as *low* as possible, not as high as possible as with the current OPEC.

And that is what we did. From shortly after the end of the war until 1973, the United States controlled the price of oil by manipulating the world market. And we could do it. We were by far the strongest economy, we produced a surplus of oil, and we had major strategic reasons for doing so.

We also controlled the price of energy at home. In 1952, we began controlling the price of natural gas and of gasoline at the pump. President Eisenhower said in his memoirs that he made two major mistakes in his Presidency. They were not firing Sherman Adams sooner, and not vetoing the energy regulation bill that was passed by the Democratic Congress in 1952.

The regulation of energy prices in the United States had a predictable effect. Remember, these prices were regulated to keep the price of energy cheap! Such regulation always has the same effect: it will stimulate demand and destimulate production. It was great while it lasted. I grew up during that period, and it was great fun driving big, fast, gas-guzzling cars, keeping our houses warm, and not worrying about energy prices or energy sources. We did that throughout the '50s, '60s, and early '70s.

But things were happening that we didn't realize. Our energy production was steadily declining while our consumption was increasing. As a result, our surplus of exported oil steadily declined. The price controls were working. Our consumption kept increasing while our production decreased.

In 1967, the inevitable happened. Our demand started to exceed our production and we became a net importer of oil, which we still are today and will be in the future. But we didn't stop controlling the price; for the next two years, we continued to dump oil on the world market whenever the price started to increase (even though we were a net importer of oil).

By 1969, the difference between our demand and production had driven our imports to a point where we couldn't afford to continue controlling prices by dumping oil on the world markets. We were forced to stop oil price controls.

It took four years, until 1973, for OPEC, and in particular Saudi Arabia, to wake up. What they discovered was that the price of oil on the spot market in Amsterdam was about $8.00 per barrel while they were being paid about $2.00 per barrel. So they decided to try selling for $6.00 per barrel, $2.00 under the spot price, to see if they could hold that price. They could do this because the United States had lost its power to control the world price of oil.

Since then, much has happened, most of which has been covered on the front pages and on the nightly news. We had the Arab boycott in the '70s, where the Arab members of OPEC boycotted the United States because of our relationship with Israel. Israel fought several real and unofficial wars with its neighbors. Iran and Iraq fought a bitter eight-year war. There was a peace agreement between Israel and Egypt and, now, potentially, with some of Israel's other neighbors. We had the Lebanon crisis. We had our diplomats kidnapped by Iran. We fought the Gulf War. And the list goes on and on.

And what happened to the price of energy and, especially, of oil while all of this was happening?

Figure 1-1 tracks the nominal well head price for oil along with the real well head price in 1993 dollars. Note that after World War II, the real price started a steady downward trend until the energy crisis

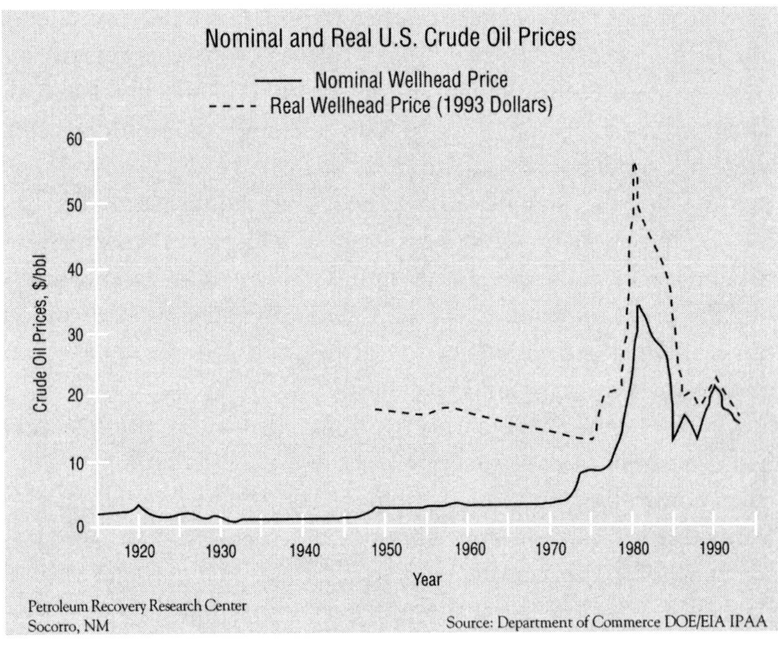

Figure 1.1

of 1973. After that, it started fluctuating as the price of energy tried to find its proper level after decades of price controls. It has now finally settled in the area of $15.00 per barrel of oil in 1973 dollars.

Thus, history shows that of all our fears, such as running out of oil or high oil prices ruining our economy, none have materialized. What has happened is that the supply today remains abundant and the price has stayed fairly steady at the level it would have been at had it been left alone starting in the '50s.

To see this from another perspective, let's look at energy and its availability from an engineering perspective.

Energy Sources

Total energy isn't something we are going to run out of. The energy we receive from the sun, for example, will last for about five billion more years, longer than there has been life on the earth. Energy will come from a variety of sources and the relative uses of the various sources will certainly vary with time. Our present dependence on oil as an energy source will undoubtedly change. However, it will not change dramatically in the near future.

The burning of hydrocarbons—in particular, the burning of oil—is generally what we mean when we get concerned about running out of energy. Unfortunately, or fortunately, depending on how one looks at the situation, oil represents a wonderful source of energy. It is abundant, fairly cheap, easily transportable, fairly safe, and has a high energy content.

However, oil does have problems. Its major sources are in areas of the world that are either hard to get to or have governments that are unstable or that are unfriendly to Western countries. Oil can make a real mess if it is spilled, particularly if it is spilled in the water. When it is burned, it consumes oxygen and generates carbon dioxide. Carbon dioxide production and the resulting potential for global warming from the greenhouse effect might be the most significant problem we will face in our energy supply situation over the next several hundred years.

All hydrocarbons, including coal and natural gas as well as oil, generate carbon dioxide when they are burned in air. They each generate carbon dioxide depending on the amount of carbon they contain. Generally, coal contains the most carbon and natural gas contains the least carbon with oil somewhere in between the two. In addition, they all contain hydrogen with trace amounts of other elements, particularly sulfur. As these hydrocarbons are burned with oxygen, the carbon in them is converted to CO_2 (carbon dioxide) and the hydrogen in them is converted to H_2O (water). The small amounts of sulfur are converted to sulfur dioxide and other oxides of sulfur. These emissions can make acid rain, and are currently removed from exhausts by various types of scrubbers (see Chapter 3 on pollution).

The current concern about global warming and the resulting greenhouse effect is serious and it must be studied further. We do not know for sure at this point if global warming is even happening. We think that it may be happening. We definitely don't know all of the effects of global warming. We don't know if the higher concentrations of carbon dioxide in the atmosphere are good or bad. It might be good for plants by allowing them to make more food using the higher CO_2 concentrations. Much more research is needed in this area.

These concerns about the future availability of energy and about the emissions from burning of fossil fuels have caused us to investigate other ways to create the energy we need. These alternatives include windmills, solar power, and electric cars, all which I will discuss below.

It is interesting to point out here that the large interest in electric-powered cars to help clean up the atmosphere will actually make the greenhouse effect worse. That is because the electricity required to charge the cars' batteries must come from somewhere. It will most likely come from a coal-burning electric power plant that emits the highest concentration of carbon dioxide of any of the three fossil fuel sources.

Note that this engineering discussion has said nothing about whether there will be enough fossil fuels to power our needs. As I will discuss later, there certainly will be enough of these fuels to meet our needs for several hundred years into the future. However, there might be other considerations, such as global warming, that will require us to change our primary sources of energy before that time.

What might some of these other sources of energy be?

The first one that comes to mind is solar power. It has the advantage of having a nearly infinite availability. Also, the earth is already receiving a steady dose with no ill effects. Its greatest disadvantage is that it arrives at the earth at a relatively low intensity level and generally in areas where we don't need it. Solar power, therefore, usually must be converted into another kind of energy before it becomes really useful to our civilization. It is most commonly converted into electricity. One way this is done is by using hydroelectric dams to capture falling water that was originally lifted into the atmosphere with solar energy. A second way is to use windmills to capture solar energy contained in the wind. A third way is to capture solar heat and light directly using solar cells or some other mechanism to convert solar radiation directly into electricity. A fourth way is to capture solar heat and use it directly for space heating and hot water heating. A fifth way is to grow things using solar energy and then burn what is grown. The burning of trees and the manufacture of alcohol for fuel are both examples of using this last method of capturing solar energy. All of these methods are more or less effective in capturing some of the solar energy falling on the earth's surface.

The problem with solar energy is that, with the exception of hydroelectric dams, capturing it is not cost-effective. Even with dams, the political difficulties in building or even maintaining them today probably makes them a poor cost-effectiveness option.

Solar energy simply does not reach the earth's surface in high enough concentration to make it cost-competitive with other forms of energy. That is not to say that it won't become competitive some day, but the prices of fossil fuels will increase substantially before that will happen. Perhaps someday, the environmental cost of carbon dioxide will drive the price of fossil fuel to the level where solar energy is cost competitive, but that remains to be seen (see sections of this chapter on economics and politics).

The second alternative energy source is nuclear power. This is a favorite of mine, obviously, because of my early career background. Nuclear power has the advantages of being abundant, of being potentially cheap, and of not polluting in the conventional sense. Its disadvantages are political. Since the accidents at Three Mile Island and Chernobyl, people are simply too afraid of nuclear power for it to be a viable source of energy in the near future. That may change, however, if global warming worsens or if something else causes fossil fuels to become unacceptable.

Nuclear energy does not contribute to global warming. It makes no carbon dioxide or any other gas. Its output is energy, waste heat that can sometimes be reused, and a very small volume of radioactive waste. It is the radioactive waste that is the problem because we haven't been able to make the political decisions necessary to enable us to safely dispose of the waste. Because of the great fear of radioactivity and of the association of "nuclear" with atomic bombs, no one wants the nuclear waste in their back yards. Even when scientists maintain that it can be handled quite safely, is very small in volume, and poses no threat to the general public, people still will not accept the waste in their neighborhood. This may be an insurmountable obstacle to the use of nuclear power.

Nuclear power and hydroelectric power are the only presently available sources of energy that are developed, are cost competitive, and do not contribute to atmospheric pollution. It never ceases to amaze me that the people who are the most concerned about our use of fossil fuels are usually the same people who reject out of hand the only two sources that can realistically replace fossil fuels in the near future: hydroelectric dams and nuclear power.

The third possible source of energy is the final development of fusion energy. This source of energy is probably far in the future. Developing fusion power is a daunting engineering task because of the extremely high temperatures and pressures involved in these reactions. When it is accomplished, someday, we will have the power of the sun available for our use in the high concentrations needed in our modern world. Because fusion power has always been twenty years or more away from viability, I think that it will be many decades before we accomplish this engineering feat. During that time, the burning of fossil fuels will continue to be our prime source of energy.

The Political Economics of Fossil Fuel Supply

Are there enough fossil fuels? Aren't we going to run out? These are perfectly natural questions to ask and be concerned about. Of course we will probably run out some day; that is the only rational answer when we consider that our planet is a finite place. But the point at which we will run out is far in the future and will occur after our energy costs and prices have risen much higher than they are today, pushing the development of other sources of energy (see the discussion on economics earlier in this chapter).

From a geologic perspective, the world is a very big place. There is the potential for fossil fuel production in much of it, but there are many areas that have been only lightly developed. Many areas of the world remain available for future development of fossil fuel production. Although few of these are in the United States, they are available elsewhere in the world.

Fossil fuels include more than just petroleum. They include coal, oil shale, tar sands, and natural gas.

We have only recently started to really use natural gas. In many parts of the world, it is flared off because it isn't worth trying to transport to a market. Coal is very abundant in the United States and in many other parts of the world. Simply stated, there are enough fossil fuels for the foreseeable future. They may not stay at their current prices, and the mix may change from oil toward natural gas or coal, but the fuels are available. The important point is that they are there at a price. Presently, the price seems to be at or near $15.00 per barrel of oil equivalent. It has been there for several years and seems likely to remain steady for many years in the future. If the price does increase, there will surely be more alternative fossil fuel energy sources available at the higher price.

The best example of this was the attempt to develop the oil shale in Colorado during the height of our panic because of the 1970's energy crisis. This very large development and ultimate failure was promoted by our government and by some very large companies. An enormous amount of money was lost and thousands of people lost their jobs and homes because of the mistaken set of assumptions that were used on the project. The assumption was that the world was running out of energy and that oil prices would surely reach $50 to $100 per barrel. At that price, the development of oil from shale becomes cost-effective. Unfortunately, in this case the world wasn't running out of oil, it just needed to be paid a fair price for it. As soon as the fair price was established at under $20 per barrel, the supply came back into balance, and the high cost of shale development projects resulted in their failure.

Once the price of oil reached a level where it made economic sense, oil (and natural gas) became available from many sources. Oil and gas came from new fields in the United States, and new developments or increases in production occurred in the north slope in Alaska, Mexico, Canada, the North Sea, the Middle East, Indonesia, Australia, Russia, Indo-China, and China. There were additional sources in South America and other parts of the world. All of this new capacity came about because the prices were fair and these countries could afford to produce the energy at the prices they were receiving. Geologically, there was plenty of oil and other types of energy. The problem wasn't engineering or geology, and never has been. The problem was economic and political, and always has been.

What were the economics and politics of the energy crisis and all that has happened since? Why did we do what we did? Whose interests did it serve? Did we intend to do what we did? These are all interesting questions. Some of them might not have complete answers, but I can put forth ideas as to why some of these things happened.

As I said earlier in this chapter, my personal belief early in my career was that energy was a finite commodity, that we were sure to run out of it, and that we would probably run out of it sooner rather than later. I held this view for most of my early career in the Navy and at Kenworth, and through the energy crisis period of the early '70s. I bought small cars, car pooled, and insulated my house just like the rest of the U.S. population. At Kenworth, we supported the 55 mph speed limit, even though it severely restricted the productivity of our trucks. I supported the development of coal hauler trucks because I believed coal would surely become a more important part of our energy mix. I didn't start changing my ideas until I had the opportunity to attend a summer management course at Stanford University in the summer of 1980.

At that course, we listened to lectures from prominent economists and educators. It was there that I first heard the history of oil that I related earlier in this chapter. (It was also there that I first heard the story that starvation in our modern world exists only where there are civil wars going on; I will discuss this more in Chapter 4).

The fundamental conclusion that I came to after the summer at Stanford was that the supply and use of energy is not fundamentally an engineering problem, but that it is an economic problem. Because of the tremendous importance of energy to the economies of the world, the economics of energy always have strong political importance. Historically, economics has always been considered in the political climate in which it exists. The politics are important.

What are the political-economic ramifications of energy? Other than food, there isn't any other commodity that is more important to our modern society than energy. Our whole civilization is built on the use of large amounts of energy. We can't change that and we shouldn't want to. This modern society is the best there has ever been. We live better, eat better, live longer, have time for recreation and the arts, and are safer than ever in history. This lifestyle, which we now have the luxury to criticize, is largely the result of our ability over the last couple of centuries to harness and use the energy sources available to us. It is such an attractive life that we and some others enjoy that people all over the world are striving to achieve some of the same for themselves.

It seems obvious, then, that a commodity as important as this would be a strong candidate for political or government control or interference. I think we all know that this has been the case. Governments all over the world have programs and systems in place that are designed to control the sourcing, distribution, and use of energy in all of its different forms. These various systems vary from outright ownership of the entire oil industry of a country, to taxing systems, to restrictions on importing or exporting oil. For example, Mexico's government owns the country's entire oil industry. Another example is that of Europe, where the taxes on gasoline are very high to discourage use. A final example is that of the United States, where we were not allowed to export Alaskan crude oil until this year.

All of these various controls affect the energy situation in the world. They do not exist in a vacuum. The entire energy market is interconnected economically on a worldwide basis. All of the political influences have an effect on the overall energy market.

Energy, just like anything else, reacts to the laws of economics. Probably the most fundamental law of economics is that there is a price for everything. Energy is no different. If people are willing to pay more for something, then more of it will be available. That certainly has been the case with oil. When the price increased, more became available. Then the price decreased because too much became available, and then the price increased again, and so on until the price eventually stabilized.

As I related earlier, the proximate cause of the energy crisis in the '70s was when the United States became unable to continue to control the price of oil worldwide. It took several years for prices to stabilize after that, and we had to fight a couple of wars (or almost wars) before they did, but they finally settled at their current level of about $15.00 per barrel.

During this time, it was politically advantageous to the United States to have a scapegoat for the energy crisis. Fortunately for the United States, OPEC came along and played this role very nicely. They controlled most of the world's oil. They raised prices at the time when we all thought we were going to run out of oil. They had a different culture than ours. They didn't like us and boycotted us and captured our diplomats. They made a fine villain. The problem is that they never were and currently aren't the controlling factor in the world energy market. There simply is too much energy available from too many other sources for OPEC to dominate.

OPEC has never been a very effective cartel. They have more problems with their own members than they have dealing with the rest of the world. Can you imagine trying to control a supply cartel where two of the members are Iran and Iraq? There has been so much cheating over the years by OPEC members that it seems like most of the reports from their meetings are about production limits to give their attempts at price control a chance of succeeding. Saudi Arabia has had to absorb the brunt of the production cutbacks because none of the other OPEC members would help.

Rather than setting prices, OPEC has usually been a price follower, staying about $2.00 under the spot price for crude oil. So, what actually has been happening since the crisis times in the '70s is the world economic markets have been setting the proper prices for energy and OPEC has been following those prices.

Another problem that OPEC had is that the higher prices for oil that started coming to pass in the '70s stimulated much more production from all over the world. Their percentage of the worldwide production started falling and they became even less able to control prices.

Now, after over twenty years, the energy markets are finally stabilizing and perhaps we are starting to make some better decisions. When we make decisions based on the belief that we will run out of energy soon or that its price will increase dramatically, those decisions are sure to be wrong. There are many decisions made in the last twenty years that were based on the false expectations of continually rising oil prices. These decisions have been very wrong and have greatly cost the people who made them. They include the following:

- President Carter decided to ration U.S. energy, which was not only not necessary, but helped cripple his presidency.
- Oil shale development projects in Colorado were undertaken.
- Many coal development projects were begun.
- The world's tanker fleet was increased in size to a point that it was too large for the world market.
- Oil field development companies grew with the assumption that there was no end to the need for such development.
- People bought sailboats when they really wanted power boats.
- Large transportation projects were started, assuming that people would stop driving their private cars.

In addition to the above supply-side changes that occurred when the price increased, there were also changes on the demand side. It turned out that demand was strongly affected by price. Again, the laws of economics prevailed. When the price went up, demand went down.

We all know what our response was. We started driving smaller cars. Fuel economy became more important than horsepower in our purchasing decision when buying a car. We insulated our houses and lowered our thermostats. We started recycling. Our factories all embarked on large projects to reduce their energy consumption.

All of this resulted in declining demand for energy just when production was being increased. And economics took over. The price came back down and finally equalized at a reasonable level that balances production and use.

Again, there were many decisions that were made based on the assumption that demand would just continue to increase and that it wouldn't be affected by price. Again, these decisions were wrong and were very costly. Some examples are:

- The large losses taken by the Washington Public Power Supply System (WHPPS), the attempt in Washington State to build five nuclear power plants simultaneously.
- The near-total end of nuclear power plant construction in the United States.
- Developments of coal and natural gas energy sources that didn't, in the end, have enough market for their products.
- The tax-supported development of solar energy, windmills, and cogeneration projects. None of these have proven to be cost-effective.
- Increased distribution systems when demand declined.
- The development of alternate fuels such as alcohol.

Summary

The conclusion from this discussion is that the assumption that we are about to run out of energy, or at least run out of oil in the near future, is simply wrong. There is little chance that we will run out or even run short of energy in the foreseeable future. There is too much available from too many varied sources for that to happen.

The real question is what are the economics and politics of the energy situation? What is the price? Where is the price going? What is that price change telling us? What are the various governments around the world doing to affect that price? The answers to those questions will give a better picture as to what is happening to energy than any engineering or geologic forecast.

What should we do or what can we expect to happen?

First, we should recognize that there is no real crisis and that our children and grandchildren will have an adequate energy supply.

Second, we should realize that if the pricing mechanism is left reasonably alone, supply and demand for energy will continue to move along with each other.

Third, we should expect the real price for energy to slowly increase over time as the cheaper sources are used up. It won't be any rapid increase, and the increases should be easily absorbed by our economy as we become more efficient in everything that we do.

Fourth, we should expect that if the price does go up, more supply will become available and demand will drop.

Fifth, we should be concerned about the greenhouse effect and global warming. We should support more research in that area.

Finally, we should make our major societal decisions with the above truths in mind. If we do, our decisions will be better, and our society and all of us in it will benefit.

2

Transportation

WITH THE EXCEPTION OF HOUSING AND FOOD, transportation is the most costly element of our modern lives. Our ability to move around our communities, our country, and our world provides one of the most important benefits of modern society. It may be the most important benefit because of how travel has allowed all of us to become closer and has lessened the barriers between various communities and cultures.

There probably hasn't been an invention since fire that has changed our lives as much as the invention of the heat engine. This was first in the form of the steam engine and was later followed by the internal combustion engine.

Before heat engines, all of our work was done by our own muscle power or by the muscle power of work animals. A small amount of work was done by windmills and water wheels, but even these inventions were only used in relatively recent times.

Transportation before heat engines was by foot, cart or carriage, or horseback in early times. Most people never traveled more than twenty miles from where they were born. At sea, wind provided the power and ships were small, slow, and could only go where the wind would take them.

Then the heat engine was invented and the industrial revolution started. Everything changed. Factories were started, cities became larger, labor changed from farms to factories, and on and on.

Part of the change came from the application of the heat engine to transportation. This was first done with the steam engine in railroads and steamships. These two applications dramatically changed the abilities of our society. People and goods could be shipped for long distances quite rapidly, and with the security that they would get where they were going with some regularity. The Western world, including Europe and North America, got an almost insurmountable lead on the rest of the world in the nineteenth century partly because they were the first to embrace these new technologies and apply them extensively to their societies.

In the latter part of the nineteenth and early part of the twentieth centuries, the internal combustion engine was developed. These engines are the now familiar gasoline and diesel engines. Later in the twentieth century, the gas turbine engine was also developed. These were the engines that made the big difference in our transportation systems, particularly in personal transportation.

The application of the gasoline engine to carts to make the personal automobile was a revolution of immense proportions. People could now go where they wanted, when they wanted, and were able to do it quickly and in reasonable comfort. It changed our life and our world forever. The further use of engines in trucks allowed the same flexibility of movement of goods that the car gave to people.

Later, the gasoline engine was installed in airplanes and our world seemed even smaller because we were able to travel from place to place dramatically faster. When the jet engine was put on the airplanes, speed increased even more and we started routinely traveling all over the world with speed and in comfort.

This transportation capability hasn't come cheaply. It is very expensive and often creates divisive political issues in our communities and countries. Far too often, we base our decisions on incorrect assumptions or wishful thinking. And when we make decisions based on false assumptions, those decisions will be wrong or, at least, won't be optimal.

When I talk about these decisions, I mean both our personal decisions and those made by the community as a whole. These decisions can range from what type of car we buy or whether or not we even have a car. They include such things as what our communities will do for public transportation, expansion or building of new airports, building new highways, and expanding existing ones—or whether they will do anything at all. These decisions all have profound affects on our lives. They will affect our taxes, our ability to move around our communities, where we will live, how we will move our goods to market, and many other aspects of our lives.

In recent times, it has become politically correct to make decisions based on the assumption that the private automobile is basically the problem and that the goal of all of our transportation decisions should be to get people out of their private cars. Unfortunately, these decisions are based on false assumptions and do not serve our communities as they deserve to be served.

The assumption that the private car is the problem started with the energy crisis of the early '70s (see Chapter 1). At that time, the private car became the symbol of our profligate lifestyle and of our excessive use of energy. Most of us believed this and went out and bought smaller cars as soon as we could. Gas mileage became one of the most important feature of cars. In doing this, we almost destroyed our own automobile industry because automobile companies couldn't change their production to small cars fast enough to meet the change in demand. Japan and Germany benefited greatly from this change and we still have a large balance of payments problem with Japan due largely to the sudden change to small cars that we made in the '70s.

Over the next twenty years, we tried to make many more changes to our transportation system to get people out of their private cars. Examples of some of these changes include:

- Adding HOV lanes to our freeways. These lanes are intended to encourage people to use public transportation or to carpool. Often these changes remove other lanes from the freeways or they prevent adding regular lanes where they are needed.

- Installing large, publicly financed rapid transit systems in our major cities. Often these systems are some form of light rail.
- Restricting the construction of new freeways in our major metropolitan areas based on the assumption that if we allow the traffic congestion to get bad enough, then people will move from their single family homes to apartments and start using public transportation.
- Making it difficult to build or expand airports to handle the increases in air travel that we are experiencing.
- Drawing up master development plans for our regions that propose people move into high-density living patterns that will support mass transit instead of live in single family homes in the suburbs.
- Encouraging new and alternative types of vehicles such as electric cars.
- Mandating fuel economy standards for our cars as well as mandating clean air standards for our cities (see Chapter 3 on pollution).

Interestingly, none of these political solutions to our transportation difficulties have worked for the basic reason that so many people really love their personal cars, and they don't intend to get rid of them or stop using them. And people are offered very little real incentive to do so, even though the politically-correct politicians and planners want them to.

The private vehicle is by far the most comfortable, practical, flexible, and probably most cost-effective form of transportation available. Most people will decide to use it when there is no real reason not to, which is what is currently happening. Lets look at the results of twenty years of intense efforts to get people out of their private cars:

- Public transportation usage has dropped significantly over the last twenty years. In fact, its use has been dropping steadily for the last seventy years.
- The use of private cars has been steadily increasing.
- We are shifting toward ownership of trucks to counteract the mandated increased costs (via various taxes and surcharges) of cars, particularly large cars.

- Our use of air travel has skyrocketed.
- In all cases where publicly supported rapid transit systems have been developed, the high costs have required the systems to have large public subsidies to survive.
- We have had to continue our large public subsidy of Amtrak to allow it to survive.
- Our automobile and energy companies are thriving.

These results show that the private automobile is the preferred mode of transportation for most people and that they are not going to stop using it. We should begin to incorporate this fact into our political decisions. There is really no economic reason for people to stop using their private cars. There is no fuel shortage, fuel is relatively cheap, and cars are comfortable and convenient. The only possible reason for not using private automobiles is because of their carbon dioxide emissions which contribute to the greenhouse effect, but the scientific evidence supporting this effect is still too vague for any rational decisions to be made by the average car user. So, people will continue to use their private cars, probably at a continuously increasing rate.

What should we do? This is a question that governments and planners are struggling with all over the world.

I think that we should first realize and accept the basic facts outlined so far in this book. If we can, maybe in the future we can make better decisions that will be more likely to result in successful solutions.

Some decisions that might come out of this realization would be the following:

- We would continue to have emission standards for our vehicles, but would discontinue our fuel economy standards. Why not let the marketplace dictate the types of cars that people buy rather than letting the government dictate a fleet mix (via taxes) that isn't what the public wants? If this change were made, we might see a shift back from trucks and vans to cars.
- We should build more highways, particularly linking our suburbs together, allowing people to choose to live in suburbs if they want.

- We should add more airport capacity in the areas where it is needed. Because of the difficulties involved in building completely new airports, this probably means expanding existing airports.
- As we improve our rapid transit systems in our urban areas, we should look at the results in a factual way. We should not predict results based on wishful thinking. Most people will continue to use their private cars. In addition, the worst congestion problems won't be getting into and out of the primary urban centers, but probably will be between suburban centers. The solution might be buses because of their great flexibility compared with rail systems.

All of these decisions must be made based on the fact that we won't be able to get people out of their private automobiles, nor should we want to. We should provide the services that private car users need as well as excellent public transport services for people who will continue to use them. And we should recognize that long-distance travel will be by air and not rail. We must provide for that need as well because it will not disappear.

3

Pollution

THE CONVENTIONAL WISDOM REGARDING the condition of our environment and our pollution is that they are bad and getting worse. Another commonly held belief is that capitalism and business are the villains in this area. Much of our society believes that various social policies and programs are necessary in order to fix the problems.

This politically correct conventional wisdom is wrong!

The facts are that pollution levels in the Western world are not getting worse, they are rapidly improving. The facts also show that the parts of the world where pollution levels are lowest and improving quickest are in the liberal western democracies. There are strong reasons for this.

Let's start again with some history. We are living in an era that is the product of the great industrial revolution of the nineteenth and twentieth centuries. The revolution resulted primarily from the invention of the heat engine, which allowed us to replace muscle power with fuel energy. The result was an enormous increase in productivity which caused corresponding enormous changes in our lives, both positive and negative. Among the positive were changes were the following:

- We were assured that we would have the ability to grow enough food for ourselves. Transportation, refrigeration, and new distribution systems changed the way we fed ourselves. Over time, we switched from growing food on our farms to shopping at the supermarket.
- Because we were able to feed ourselves with fewer and fewer people working on farms, many people started moving into cities to find other work. These new jobs allowed us to make things for other people, to provide services for them, and, for some of us, to spend time on intellectual pursuits.
- From the industrial revolution to the present, our cumulative knowledge base has grown enormously. Because of the industrial revolution, many people have had the ability and money to spend time learning and inventing. All of this increase in knowledge has had great effects on our lives. Imagine what life would be like without things like refrigeration, automobiles, airplanes, electricity, pasteurization, penicillin, the polio vaccine, running water, flush toilets, central heat and air conditioning, telephones, television, motion pictures, radio, or computers. These things became possible because we freed ourselves from the drudgery of feeding ourselves using only our own muscle power, or that of animals.

Not all of the effects of the industrial revolution were positive. Our wars became much worse because technological advances were applied to increase military efficiency. The tank in World War I and the airplane in World War II are prime examples of this. In addition, as we moved into higher concentrations in cities, new problems of housing, crime, the workplace, and pollution arose. These problems had plagued us forever, but became more pronounced in the tight quarters of city living.

Perhaps the most profound effect of the industrial revolution has been the worldwide explosion of the human population. The world population has grown exponentially since the beginning of the industrial revolution. This is such a profound and important change that I will devote an entire chapter to it later in the book (see Chapter 4).

The large increase in population is one of the main reasons that pollution has become such a large concern in our modern society. There is no question that more people put more requirements and stress on our environment, and one of those stresses is pollution. It is easy to blame pollution on the Western world and on the Western lifestyle. Although that might be a good place to start, pollution is much worse in the socialist economies of the world where people have not had the ability to speak out about and influence the environments in which they live.

In fact, in the Western world, we generally have had the environment and pollution levels that we wanted or were willing to tolerate. The pollution levels have changed dramatically over recent years, generally for the better.

Let's look at the three main areas of pollution concerns: air, water, and land.

Air pollution is—and probably should be—the pollution that we are most concerned about. Our very life itself depends upon the health of the great ocean of air that we live in. Our atmosphere provides us with the oxygen that we need to live; regulates the earth's temperature, making it livable for humans; and protects us from the high radiation levels of outer space.

One fact about the industrial revolution is that it is fueled by the burning of fossil fuels. That is a simple statement, but might not be well understood by most people. Most of the energy that we use in our modern world comes from the burning of oil and its derivatives, and from the burning of coal, natural gas, and wood. We also use energy from nuclear power, hydroelectric dams, solar sources such as wind power, from muscle power. The vast majority of our energy comes from the combustion (or burning) of some material, which consists primarily of burning a combination of carbon and hydrogen with oxygen in our atmosphere. The end products are carbon dioxide and water.

The carbon, hydrogen, carbon dioxide, and water cycles represent the basic chemical cycles that support life on our blue-water planet. All living things burn sugars (which are carbon-hydrogen compounds) with oxygen to create the energy that they need to survive. In return, the green plants on the land and in the oceans take the carbon dioxide in the atmosphere, combine it with water, and use the energy of the sun to recreate sugars so the cycle can continue. This is a natural, continuous, process that has been going on for as long as there has been life on the earth.

The potential problem with our effects on the earth is that we are burning more carbon hydrogen compounds than ever before, which is causing the concentration of carbon dioxide in our atmosphere to increase. This increase might or might not be a problem for us. (This is the only problem covered in this book that I am personally concerned about.)

The increase in carbon dioxide has both positive and negative effects on our atmosphere. The positive effects are that it is a primary chemical source for the green plants. As the carbon dioxide concentration increases in the atmosphere, the productivity of green plants should increase, allowing us to grow more food per plant. In fact, this may ultimately limit the increase of the carbon dioxide concentration in the atmosphere.

A more significant problem is that the increase of carbon dioxide in the atmosphere might ultimately lead to a general increase in global temperature. This is called the greenhouse effect. It is the result of carbon dioxide allowing light energy from the sun through the atmosphere, and then restricting heat energy radiating from the earth from escaping back into outer space. It acts just like a gardener's greenhouse.

The concern is that global warming could have negative effects on our lives. Weather patterns may be altered, changing the areas where foods can be grown and possibly causing the polar ice caps to melt, raising the levels of the world's oceans. We currently do not know if there will even be any effects or if the carbon dioxide level increases will be good or bad. More research is needed in this area.

Over time, if we find that global warming is a serious concern, then we will have to make very radical changes in our lives. Because such a large portion of our energy comes from the fossil fuel burning, any move away from that could cause severe ramifications. Energy sources that don't require burning consist of only nuclear, hydroelectric, and solar power. In the future, we may figure out how to harness the fusion reaction and that will be another source of energy, but that is many decades away. In the meantime we will have to continue to burn fossil fuels and to continue our research on global warming.

We have either corrected *all* other types of air pollution or we know scientifically how to correct them. That is a very strong statement that is generally not believed. An absolute fact is that the air quality in the United States is better now than it has been before in this century and is continuing to improve.

Please refer to Figures 3-1 and 3-2 for examples of how our controls on air pollution have worked since they began in the 1970s. The charts show increasing levels of pollution from 1940 to 1970 and then rapidly dropping or stabilizing levels since then.

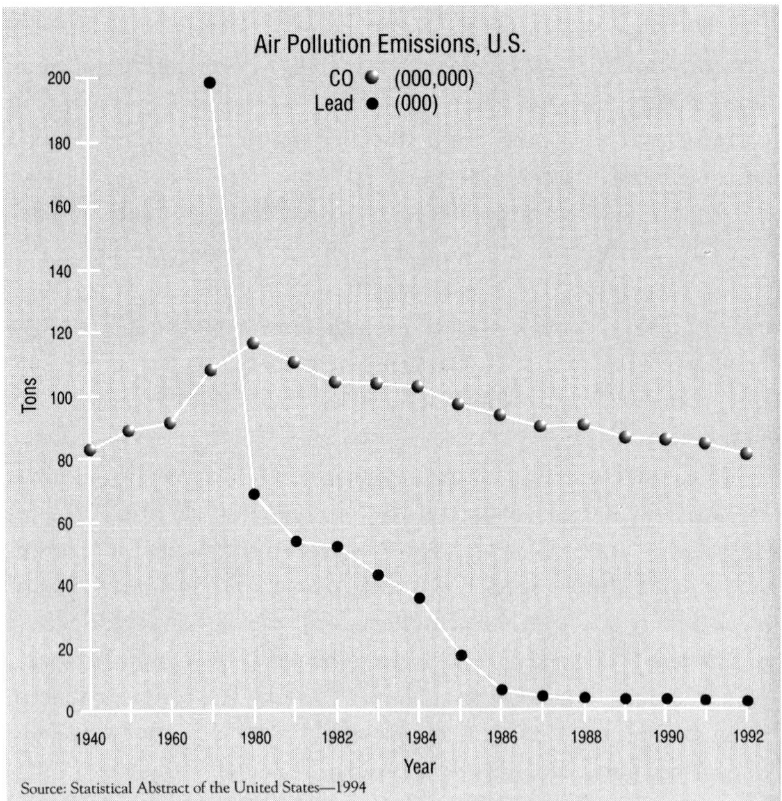

Figure 3.1

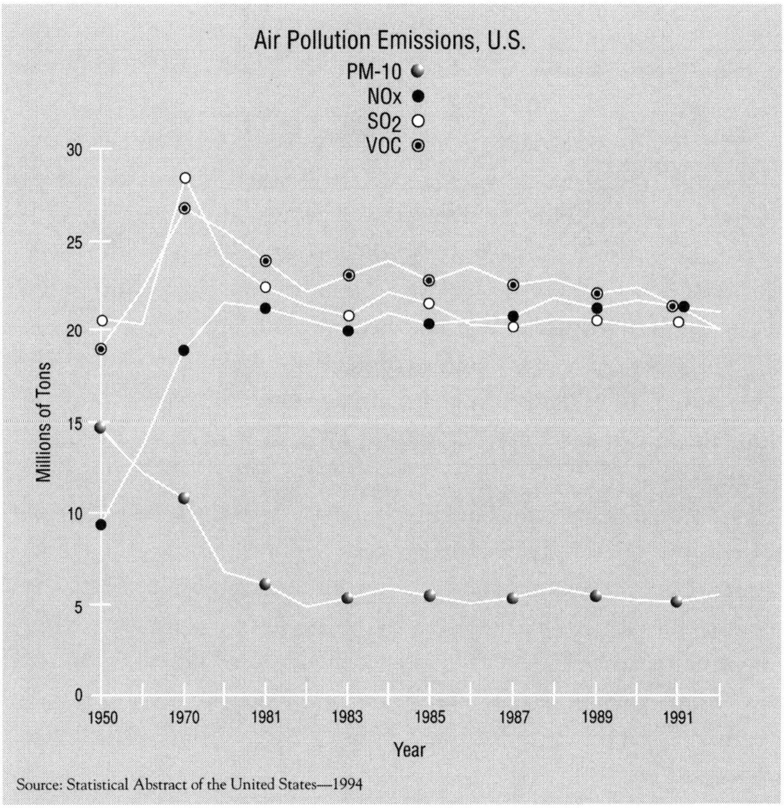

Figure 3.2

The technology and the political decisions made over the last quarter century have worked. We should recognize this and congratulate ourselves. We should also understand what worked, why it worked, what it cost, and what we should do in the future to continue our successes.

Between 50 and 150 years ago, prosperity in a community was equated with the amount of smoke that came from the community's factories. Pictures taken during that time period invariably emphasize the amount of black smoke coming from the smoke stacks that were shown. Our air became very polluted. Disease became rampant in large communities. Smog became unbearable. It wasn't a pretty picture by today's standards. At the same time, the use of automobiles and trucks increased dramatically, also contributing to the large and increasing levels of air pollution. This happened all over the world.

About fifty years ago, people in the western democracies began to become concerned and demanded that something be done about the levels of air pollution. The United States, and especially California, took the lead in starting to make the changes that were needed. California had a special problem because the pollution levels in the Los Angeles basin had become so high.

The first step was to begin to understand the cause of the pollution so that we could begin to formulate some solutions. Air pollution contains many different things, most of which are a result of combustion.

Carbon dioxide is the largest volume waste product. As I discussed earlier, it is a naturally occurring gas in our atmosphere and, in fact, required by green plants for making the food that we all need. The concern about carbon dioxide is what its effect on the atmosphere might be in higher concentrations; it might cause global warming.

Other gases might be more of a problem, but there are engineering or technical solutions for all of them. Some of the most important are:

- ***Oxides of sulfur***. See Figure 3-2. These result mainly from the burning of coal that contains high concentrations of sulfur. Oxides of sulfur are an atmospheric problem because they are acidic and cause acid rain and deterioration of our buildings, artwork, and lakes. The solution to the sulfur problem is to burn low-sulfur coal and to put scrubbers on the exhausts of coal plants. These are expensive solutions, but our society has been willing to spend the money. Another solution is to substitute low-sulfur fuels, such as natural gas, for the coal. This has happened throughout the world; the reduction of air pollution in London and Pittsburgh are among the most prominent examples.
- ***Oxides of nitrogen***. See Figure 3-2. These result from the oxidation of naturally occurring nitrogen in the atmosphere when it is involved in another hydrocarbon combustion process.

These compounds are the primary component of smog, particularly smog that comes from cars. The solution to the problem of these pollutants has been to more carefully control the combustion process. This is why our car engines have become so complicated and why we have catalytic converters on our cars. These technical improvements are expensive, but they have worked. Again, we have been willing to incur the additional costs in order to have clean air. The most prominent example of this program's success has been the Los Angeles basin. The improvement in the air pollution levels in Los Angeles in the last quarter of a century has been astounding.

- ***Freon.*** Freon has been identified as detrimental to the earth's ozone layer. The ozone layer serves to protect us from excessive ultraviolet radiation from the sun. Our society made a quick decision to control the use of Freon, which caused a significant increase in cost in cooling and refrigeration.
- ***Particulate.*** See Figure 3-2. Another form of atmospheric pollution is particulate matter. It also is a result of combustion. It is often formed when the burning isn't complete or a fuel with an high concentration of carbon is used. The biggest problems here are wood stoves, the burning of coal, and outdoor burning. Again, controls have been put on many of the particulate matter sources and their contribution to air pollution has been reduced.

There are many other chemical gases that can be of concern. We are now able to identify and place controls on them. Again, these often are costly decisions, but our society has the means and the desire to make them. In recent years, there hasn't been a chemical that is an atmospheric concern that we haven't been willing to correct.

The basic message of this discussion on air pollution is that our air is clean and is getting cleaner. Our society has decided that it is willing to pay for clean air and has passed laws and regulations intended to insure that we keep a clean atmosphere. In the liberal western democracies, enough funding has been available to pay for these changes. In the third world and in the former socialist countries, unfortunately, there isn't enough funding to pay for the clean-ups. The worst pollution conditions are generally found in those countries.

Our action should be to continue our efforts to keep our own air clean while helping the third world create enough wealth to be able to afford cleaning up their own countries. What we have been doing for the last quarter century has worked. We should recognize this so that we know how to continue.

Water pollution has a similar history to air pollution. Fifty years ago and before, we built our factories on the shores of rivers and lakes and just dumped wastes directly into the water. The pollution became very serious before it woke us up. Perhaps the best example was when the Cayuga River in Cleveland caught on fire. That event got people's attention.

Since then, we have learned what has to be done. We have been willing and able to pay the costs for these cleanups, and they have worked. The Cayuga River has been cleaned up. Lake Erie has been cleaned up. The Hudson River is coming back. Lake Washington in the Seattle area has been cleaned up. And many other bodies of water have had similar successes.

The solution to water pollution is to not put pollutants into the water. Obviously, the solution isn't so simple. Many people in the world seem to think that there is so much water that the little amount of pollution add won't make any difference.

Those attitudes are changing, however. Younger people certainly have a different attitude about water pollution than did earlier generations. Even the larger companies who may have polluted in the past are changing their ways. As shown in Figure 3-3, our level of oil-polluting incidents has dropped dramatically in the last few years. Again, our emphasis on pollution, coupled with our ability to pay the costs, has allowed us to steadily clean up our water.

Various forms of land pollution have had a similar history to air and water. In the past, little thought was given to the long-term effects of how we handled our wastes. Just as we did with our air and water, we simply dumped our solid and liquid wastes wherever it was easiest.

Our dumps often were poorly located, and there was no control over what was put into them. Individually, we often dumped our wastes out behind the garage or dumped them down the sewer. These actions resulted in contamination of numerous areas in the world, many of which have yet to be cleaned up.

But, again, attitudes have changed. Our landfills are much more sophisticated now and our individual behaviors have changed. Recycling is now very common. Service groups now regularly clean up our highways. Most of us wouldn't dream of pouring used oil down a storm drain anymore. Our land environment is not getting worse and is steadily being cleaned up.

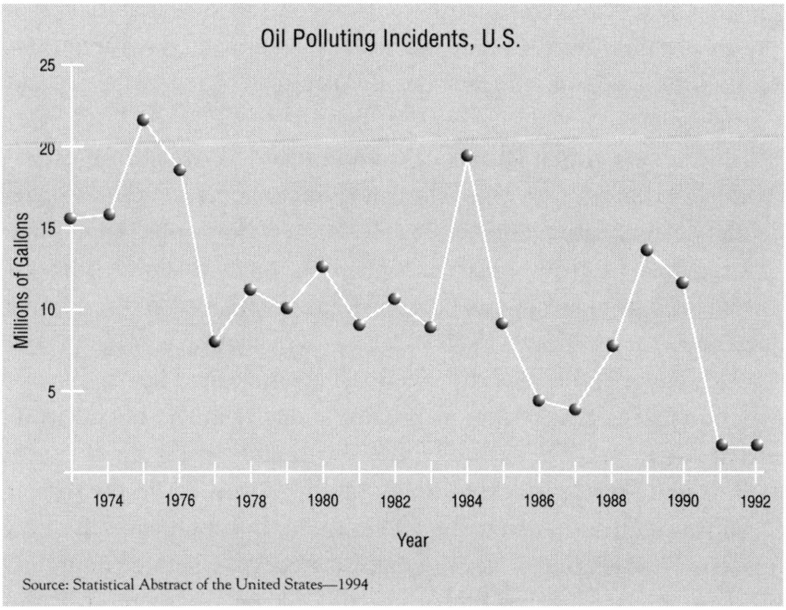

Figure 3.3

Again, the costs are high. Society must be able and willing to pay the costs. It seems that the liberal western democracies are willing and able to do so. It hasn't been easy though. Individuals, businesses, and government often resist cleaning up pollution caused by someone else in a different era. It is hard for them to understand why they are required to pay to clean up a gasoline station site when it was contaminated thirty or forty years ago by someone else. It also is hard for people to understand why they must pay for the cleanup of a large government site like Hanford when it was contaminated by bomb production of the '40s and '50s. These are the costs that must be borne in order to clean up the pollution of the past.

The good news, though, is that we are not creating new problems. The technology, the laws, and the attitudes of our society are preventing that. The new attitude is that pollution is just not acceptable. Our housing, our businesses, and our infrastructure all reflect that change.

The results of these changes over the last quarter century have been dramatic. My family lives in the Seattle area. Seattle has a completely restored lake that in the 1950s had been nearly lost before the community decided to clean it up. It is now a recreational bonanza for the community, with major fish runs, too many geese, and nesting eagles.

There are similar stories in communities all over the Western world. London no longer has killer smog since it stopped burning high-sulfur coal for heating, the Los Angeles basin no longer has killer smog since it enacted strong emission controls on cars, Pittsburgh has converted itself from a smoky city of steel mills to a high-tech center since it cleaned up its air, the Hudson River once again has fish, and the Cayuga River and Lake Erie have both been cleaned up.

The fact is that pollution is being reduced in the liberal western democracies. They have both the will and the means to do so. Unfortunately, this isn't the case in the third world or in the former socialist countries. Again, the will is there, but the means are not. It seems that economic development is necessary before communities are able to develop both the will and the means to clean up their environment.

Our action, therefore, should be to continue with what is working in our own communities while doing what we can to encourage economic development in the rest of the world. This will enable them to also benefit from the results of a cleaner environment. We also need to continue our research in two areas that might ultimately be the most important: the global warming effect of carbon dioxide, and the development of fusion power as an ultimate source of basic power for our civilization.

4

Population

EVER SINCE MALTHUS PUBLISHED his *Essay on the Principle of Population* in 1798, the conventional wisdom has been that our rapidly growing population was sure to outstrip its ability to feed itself. It seemed intuitively obvious that the earth had a finite size and so we were sure to eventually expand to the point where the earth simply could not support all of us. In recent years we have expanded that argument to include all of the resources of the earth. We believe and are coached to believe that humans are growing in numbers too quickly for the earth to be able to continue to support us all.

The reality of the matter is that none of these doomsday scenarios have come to pass. What has happened? The basic element missing in all the scenarios is that not enough credit is given to the ingenuity of the human mind. Ever since the industrial revolution began, the improvements in the various areas that needed to support ourselves have kept ahead of the continually rising population.

The world currently produces plenty of food to feed its entire population. In many parts of the world, particularly in the liberal western democracies, there is a great surplus of food production, and governments often create subsidies and/or price controls to protect farmers from their own overproduction.

The parts of the world where hunger and starvation occur often coincide with internal political strife or a civil war. In these countries, the warring parties may believe it is in their best interest to starve their own population intentionally. It is vitally important for the rest of the world to understand this and not to react to these war caused starvation stories by believing that our own food growing and distribution systems are faulty.

Another very interesting development is that a country's population growth starts to slow down as the country becomes more prosperous and more politically liberal. This phenomenon is now occurring in most of the liberal western democracies. When migration is eliminated as a variable, most of the countries of western Europe and North America, as well as Japan, are actually experiencing very slow or negative population growth.

These are very interesting trends. First, there is plenty of food. Second, hunger exists where there are civil wars. And third, population stabilizes where there is prosperity and liberal democracy. We should understand why all of these conditions exist.

Why is there plenty of food? This is an interesting question. It doesn't seem intuitively obvious why we have been able to continuously improve our food supply in order to feed our greatly increasing population. In fact, we have increased our food production faster than our population has increased (see Figure 4-1). How can that be? The answer has to be in the ingenuity of the human mind.

First of all, we could not do it if we were not farming. Natural production has no hope of keeping up with rapidly growing population. We can see this in all areas where we still hunt for our food. The exploitation of wild fish in the oceans is a prime example of how hunting just can't keep up. In the areas where we can farm the fish, however, they are a cheap and reliable source of food.

Our exploitation of the great whales is another good example. We have now realized that we can't continue to hunt wild animals as a source of food for an ever-increasing population. Many of our new regulations and controls recognize this fact and many formerly endangered species are now making a comeback. We must continue

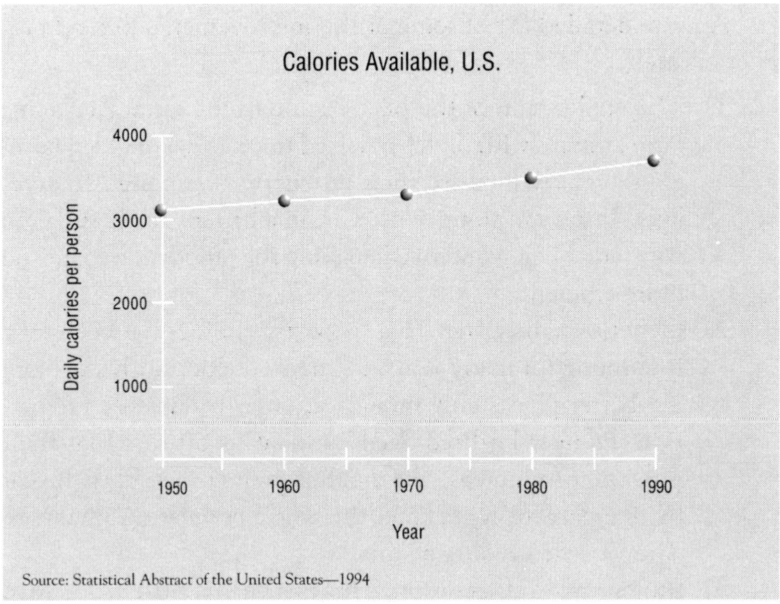

Figure 4.1

to recognize the real production limits of wild stocks and harvest only what they can supply. Salmon in the Pacific Northwest and cod on the great banks of the Atlantic are prime examples of wild stocks that could not handle the continuously increasing harvests driven by our larger population and more efficient technology.

But farming has worked. We have continuously been able to stay ahead of demand when we were able to apply our efforts to farming. There are technological, political, and economic reasons for these successes. We should understand these reasons so we can ensure and have confidence that the successes will continue in the future.

The technological reasons for these successes include improved farming methods, better farm plants and animals, more automation and power equipment, and better irrigation, storage and refrigeration methods, distribution systems, and transportation. These are all undergoing continuous improvement and will most likely continue to see long-term improvements.

A more detailed list of some of the improvements in food production are:

1) The application of the heat engine to the farm. Replacing farm animals with diesel-powered tractors has enabled farmers to greatly increase their production from a given acreage. Tractors, along with the machinery they pull, are constantly being improved, making the production more and more efficient.
2) Genetic engineering. This "new" technology has been used in farming for many years. Farmers are constantly developing better plants and animals in order to increase production. Pioneer Hi-Bred Seeds' annual report says that their mission is to increase the yield of their corn seed each year by one percent more than the world population increases. They are succeeding at this.
3) Storage and refrigeration. This has been a little recognized but profound advancement in making food available to our growing population. With modern technology, we can store food for long periods and transport food for long distances. This, possibly more than anything else, has had enormous effects on the availability of food all around the world. It is probably the main reason that hunger does not have to exist anywhere in the world as long as the political climate will allow food distribution.
4) Transportation and distribution. These have changed enormously, particularly in the developed world. We now don't give a second thought to having fresh fish in Kansas City in the winter, fresh beef in New York, and fresh strawberries in Seattle in the winter. Fresh apples are available all year long. We can ship grain halfway around the world with large ships. These improvements in transportation and distribution, which we now take for granted, have made a larger quantity and greater variety of food available to people all over the world. The absence of these capabilities in much of the third world and the formerly communist world is one of the main reasons that their quality of life is lower than it is in the developed world.

A key point is that the technologies applied in the developed world are available for use in the developing world when their economics and politics allow. Enormous increases in production are possible just from applying what we already know elsewhere in the world.

When we understand the technological reasons for our continuing abundance of food supplies, we can begin to understand why the doomsayers over the last two hundred years have been wrong. Given the opportunity and the incentive, the human mind is fully capable of finding ways to continue to improve food production to feed the increases in population. This argument can also apply to the other things that we need to support our civilization (see the chapter on energy).

But technical solutions do not exist in a vacuum. There always are political and economic considerations that have strong effects on our societies.

As discussed earlier, it is a fact that starvation in the world exists where there are wars being fought. Somalia, Cambodia, Bosnia, and other countries around the world that have the worst cases of hunger and starvation and all are involved in wars. It is the wars that cause hunger and starvation, not any technological reason indicating that the world cannot feed itself. It is important to recognize this so we can work to fix the actual problem and not a fictitious one. The problem is not that we can't grow enough food for ourselves, but that we don't allow food to reach the other side during a war. It is a political, not a technological problem, as are most of the other situations discussed in this book.

Besides wars, the other political problem is that most managed economies in communist or socialist states have severely damaged their farming economies. They have done this in several ways, but most of the damage has been the result of completely misreading human nature. Of all the things that we do to support ourselves, farming is perhaps the most independent and difficult. Consequently, it responds to incentives and to returns for the hard work done by the individual on their own land. When farms are collectivized or when the returns go to people other than those who do the work, then productivity invariably drops.

The examples of this are legion: Russia under Stalin, China under Mao, and Cuba under Castro. Each of these countries had been large producers of food before the forced collectivization of the communist regimes. After communism, not only did their production fall steeply, but the governments felt they had to kill many of the farmers in order to get the rest of them to perform. This mistaken policy is one of the great tragedies of our times, resulting in untold millions of people starving or being killed.

The next example isn't as brutal as the Communist regimes, but just as unproductive. The well-meaning socialist countries tried to collectivize farming using peaceful means. Although they didn't kill as many people, they did badly damage their countries' agricultural productivity. These policies were followed and failed in India, most of Africa, and most of South America.

The political reasons for these policies were usually rooted in leaders trying to remain popular with their large urban populations. The leaders took control of pricing and distribution of food supplies in their countries to keep the prices in cities low. These policies had predictable effects. Consumption and movement to cities was stimulated while production and living on farms was curtailed. As a result, many of these countries became unable to feed themselves.

The West then moved in with massive shipments of food to help feed the starving in these areas. We were made to feel guilty because we had such plenty while people in other countries were starving. We thought we must have been doing something wrong because the world seemed to be running out of food.

But then an amazing thing happened. Communism was shown to be the sham that it was and the other socialist countries began to realize that their policies were not working. In China, Russia, India and other countries, people were allowed to grow their own food on their own land. Economic incentive was put back into the food production process.

The predictable happened. Food production soared and these formerly dependent countries were suddenly able to feed themselves again. What had been working in the Western world for several hundred years was now working just as well in other countries.

These changes occurred all over the world in the '80s and '90s. Country after country made these changes, resulting in major economic shifts. Previously exporting countries have had to work hard to maintain their export markets as other countries have been able to reduce imports and start exporting again.

To summarize, enough food is being produced and hunger is not necessary as long as politics allow food to be produced and distributed. The world needs to understand that liberal western democracies, in which farmers are allowed to prosper from the fruits of their labor, and capitalism are the systems that have worked best in supporting our growing population.

The third interesting factor relating to population growth is that it seems to slow, and actually reverse, when societies and economies become prosperous. See Figures 4-2, 4-3, and 4-4.

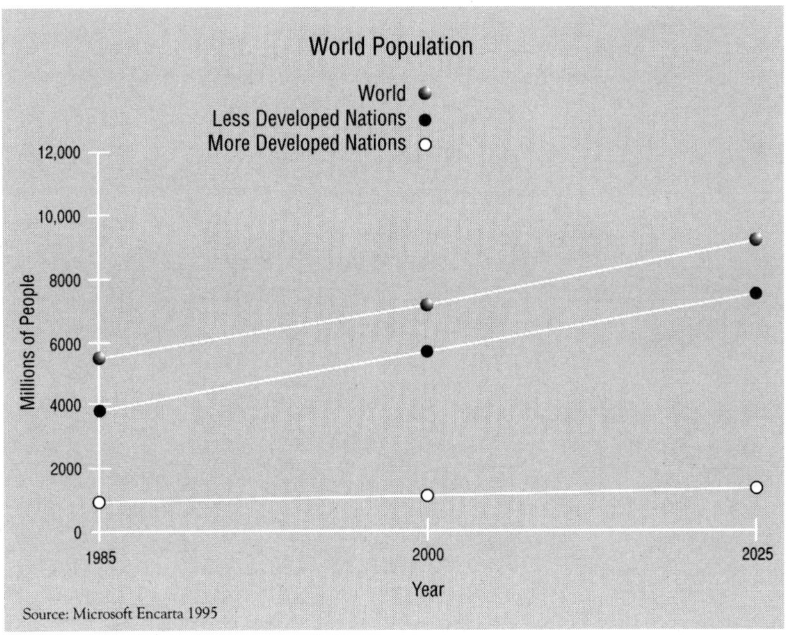

Figure 4.2

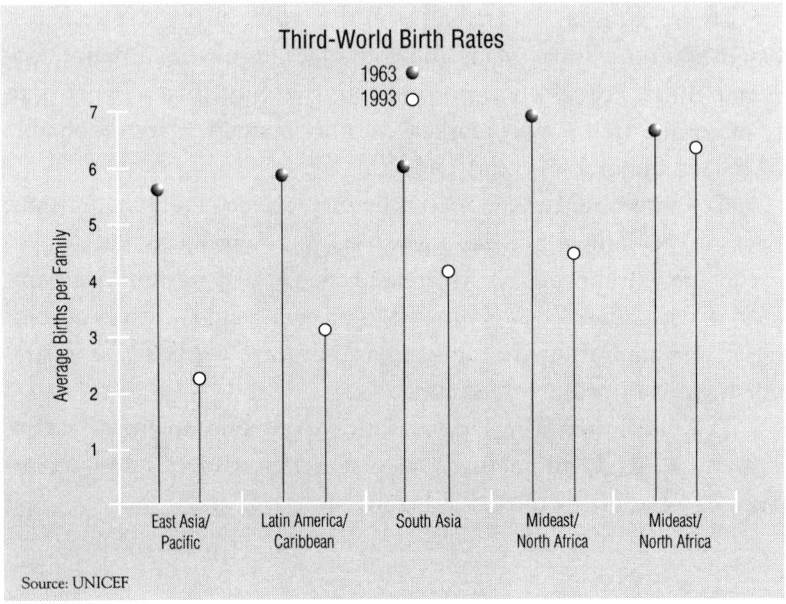

Figure 4.3

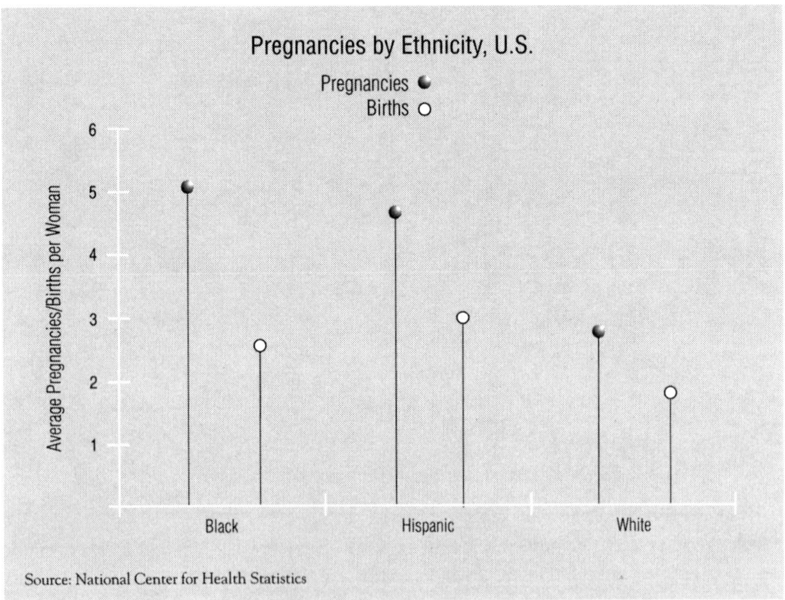

Figure 4.4

This is happening throughout the developed world. Population from the existing base (without the immigration factor) is actually decreasing in several western countries. The population growth occurring in the world today is concentrated almost entirely in the developing world, which can least afford to support it.

Several factors are contributing to this phenomenon. They include economic changes in western societies, the liberal state of their politics, the changing status of women, and the societal factors that exist in the developing countries.

For logical reasons, it seems that when a society's economic status improves, the average family size decreases. We can understand this by realizing that many of us feel we don't need or can't afford as many children in our modern societies as previous generations could. In the Western world today, children must be taken care of and educated for a much longer period than they did in the past. It is becoming necessary for people to be educated in college just to be prepared to exist and compete productively in our modern communications society. Parents must be able to support their children for over twenty years to fully prepare them for this task. Compare this with the situation a century ago, or even in much of the developing world today, where children started to help on the farm before they were ten years old.

At the same time, politics and technology have been changing. On the political front, the role of women in the Western world has been changing rapidly. Women have joined as somewhat equal partners with men in many areas of political and economic life where they were previously excluded. These areas include education, politics and business. While they still are not equal to men in all areas, their participation in the overall political and economic arenas of the Western world has definitely seen great increases in the last century. There are now more women attending college in the United States than men! (See Chapter five.)

Joining in the political-economic life of their societies has strongly influenced women's decisions about their lives. They are deciding to have fewer children and to have them later in life. Technological changes have helped women make these changes. For example, birth control is readily available and safe, so women now have real control over their child-bearing decisions.

As a result of these changes, prosperous and educated western families are having fewer children and are having them later, which has stopped the population growth or explosion in these societies. In fact, this may show that population growth might be self-limiting if societies can become economically prosperous and politically liberal. Providing women with this level of control seems to one of the key elements.

Compare that with the situation in the developing countries, where economic incentives still exist to have large families and women are still tightly controlled by their societies. They often have socialist governments that have removed incentives for farming, attracting large numbers of people into the cities. And they are often at war. These are the areas where there is a population problem, not in the Western world.

To summarize this chapter, we do not have a population problem, per se. We are well able to feed and take care of ourselves if we are given a chance. We do, however, have a political-economic problem: much of the world is following political and economic policies that do not help the situation and in fact make it worse.

The world has to recognize that farmers must be given the opportunity to make a reasonable return on their investment of labor and capital. Secondly, women must be given a more equal role in their societies. Thirdly, economic growth must occur in all parts of the world so that people can make individual life decisions that contribute to the leveling out of population growth.

When all of these things happen, it appears that population growth will cease to be a problem for the world and that it will stabilize at an easily sustainable level. Note that none of these changes are technological- or resource-based. They are all political, economic, or social. And all of them can be accomplished if we make the correct decisions in our political, economic, and personal lives.

5

Education

THE CONVENTIONAL WISDOM AS WE NEAR the end of the twentieth century is that education in the United States, particularly in Kindergarten through twelfth grade (K–12), is bad and is getting worse. This isn't completely true.

There are many social, political, and economic facts that affect our education system, our perception of it, and its success. These facts include the following:

- Our test scores seem to be declining, compared both with historical standards and with certain other countries.
- An increasingly larger portion of our population is attending college.
- An increasingly larger portion of our minority population is attending college.
- Our graduation rates from high school and college continue to increase.
- Both political parties have political reasons for criticizing our schools.
- The United States wins most of the Nobel Prizes.

- The United States leads the world in most high-tech developments.
- Women in the United States are continually increasing their participation in our economy.
- Violence in schools seems to be more prevalent.

With the exception of test scores and violence—along with our nagging suspicion that our kids don't know as much history, geography, grammar, and spelling as we did—most of the above items support the argument that our education system is not broken and is, in fact, doing a reasonably good job.

We ask too much of our education system beyond educating our children. We ask it to accomplish many social goals as well. We ask it to substitute for family failures. We ask it to babysit our children while we attend to our work responsibilities. On top of it all, we usually don't give the system enough resources to accomplish these tasks.

The result of these conflicting requirements and expectations is that although our education system is trying to do the best job it can, it is perceived by many to be failing. Much of this perception is political in nature. It is in both of our major political parties' best interest to criticize our education system. The Republicans want to enhance private education and obtain public funding for private education through vouchers or a similar system. The Democrats have a strong internal influence from the teachers' unions and, therefore, want to obtain additional funding for public education. All of these goals can be enhanced if the point is made that the existing public schools are not doing the job. The Republicans can point out that public schools should be replaced and the Democrats can make the point that we need more funding for public schools. Neither has any vested interest in saying that our public schools are doing just fine.

Another political force against our schools is a result of our attempt to integrate our country through our education system. Forced busing has had major effects on our public schools over the last forty years, not all of which have been positive. Probably many of the problems we now see in our public schools can be traced to this forced integration over the last thirty to forty years. On the other hand, many of the improvements in the performance of minorities can probably also be traced to the integration process.

Politics aside, exactly how well are our schools really doing? There are many conflicting and interesting facts that we can review in an attempt to answer this question.

First, let's look at how the United States is doing in its technology leadership position. Few would argue that the United States has taken the lead in many, if not most, of the significant technological innovations in the half century since World War II. These include the transistor, the computer, the jet airplane, the birth-control pill, genetic engineering, computer software, space travel, farm production, and many others.

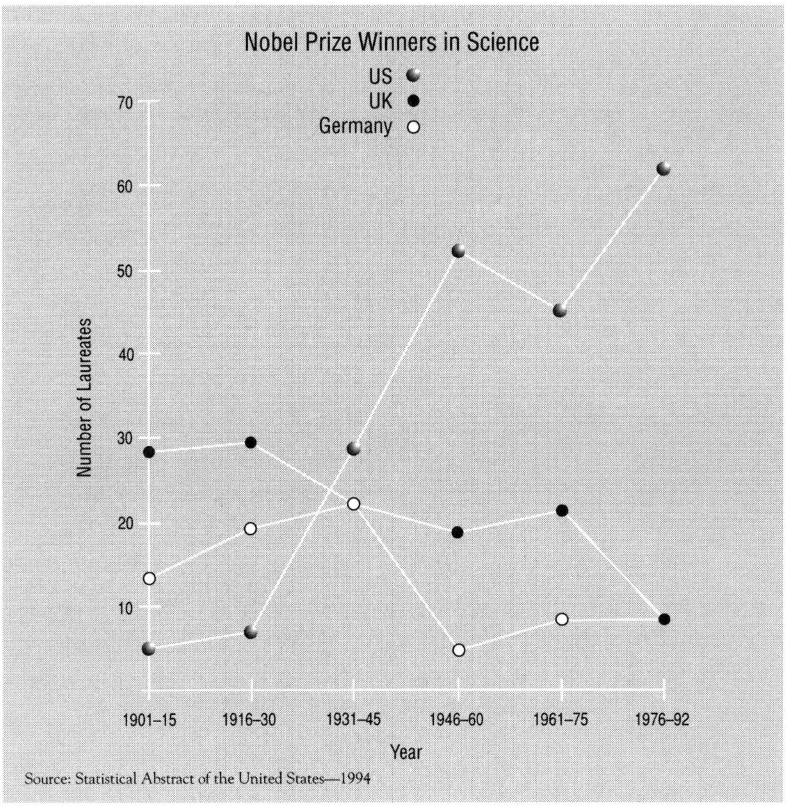

Figure 5.1a

This leadership is reflected in the number of Nobel prizes that are awarded annually in scientific fields. Figures 5-1a and 5-1b show the number of Nobel prizes awarded to scientists from various countries during fifteen-year periods in this century. The most striking feature of these charts is the emerging dominance of the United States after World War II. The U.S. share of Nobel prizes has increased from 6 percent and 30 percent in the period before the war to more than 60 percent in the most recent fifteen-year period. At the same time, the percentage of awards earned by our primary competitor countries has steadily declined. Germany received only 8 percent of the awards in the most recent period and since the early 1900s, Japan has received less than 5 percent.

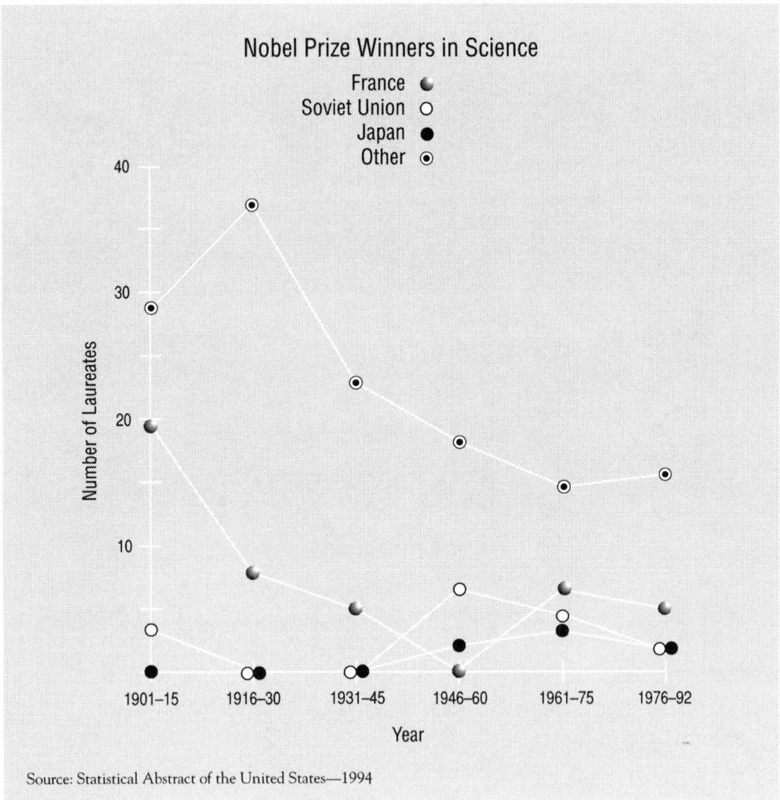

Figure 5.1b

Clearly, the U.S. education system must be doing something right if this is the case. The people who have won these awards are individually honored, so what we really should understand is why they are in the United States, what prompted them to do research, and how much their education has affected their lives. We also must understand that these people received their basic education thirty to sixty years ago. This positive trend in U.S. Nobel prizes might only be showing how good our schools were as far back as the '30s.

This trend does show some positive aspects of science in the United States. The United States is obviously able to attract, train, and retain people who are capable of winning these prizes. Some of this is due to our freedom, which attracts people from around the world, particularly those who are oppressed. The United States also has what is regarded as the premier higher education system in the world. We attract high-caliber students from all over the world to attend our institutions of higher learning, and many of these students remain in the United States. We also have many opportunities for research and development. Many of our companies make significant investments in research, our colleges and universities are unmatched in their research, and our government provides substantial support.

These are probably the real reasons why we receive so many Nobel prizes, and they also do not support the argument that our education system is broken. In fact, they support the argument that it is doing quite well.

A second way to look at our education is to look at how our students are doing, in particular, how many are graduating and going on to college? Figure 5-2 shows the high school graduation rates for whites and blacks over the last thirty-three years. Its dramatic upward trend is obvious. In 1960, 43 percent of whites and 20 percent of blacks graduated from high school. In 1993, that rate had risen to 80 percent for whites and 68 percent for blacks. This in an increase of 86 percent for whites and of 240 percent for blacks.

This is an astounding result. It certainly does not support the argument that the education system is broken, but rather that it is doing a tremendous job. The system at least is graduating more of its students.

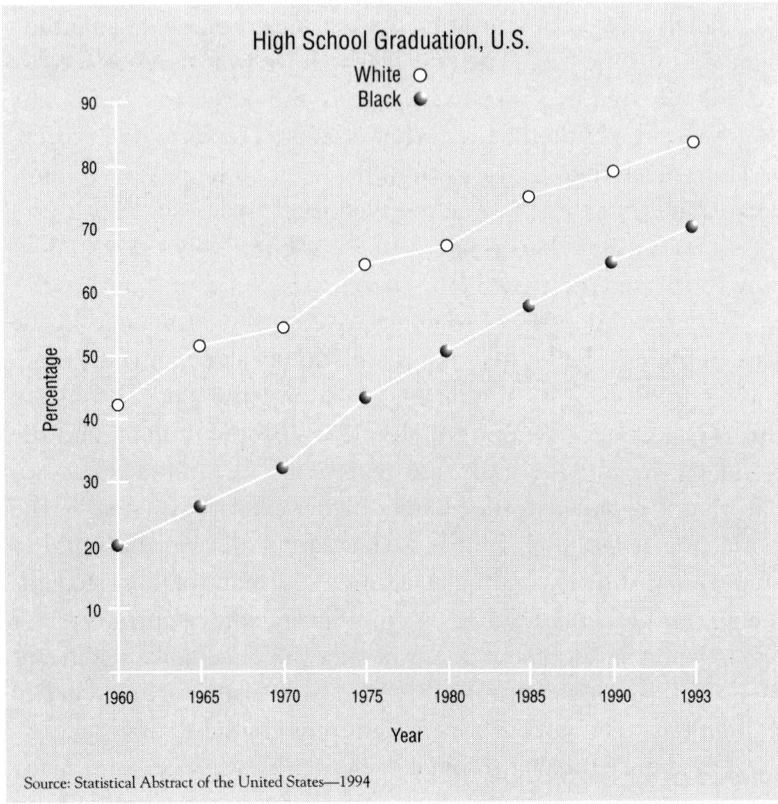

Figure 5.2

Where are these graduates going after high school? Figure 5-3 shows the percentage of high school graduates who have completed one year or more of college. This percentage has also increased dramatically over the last thirty-three years. In 1960, 41 percent of white and 32 percent of black high school graduates attended some college. By 1992, that had increased to 66 percent of whites and 52 percent of blacks. This is an increase of 61 percent for whites and 62 percent for blacks.

This data shows that over the last third of a century, we have dramatically increased both high school graduation rates and the percentage of high school graduates who have attended college.

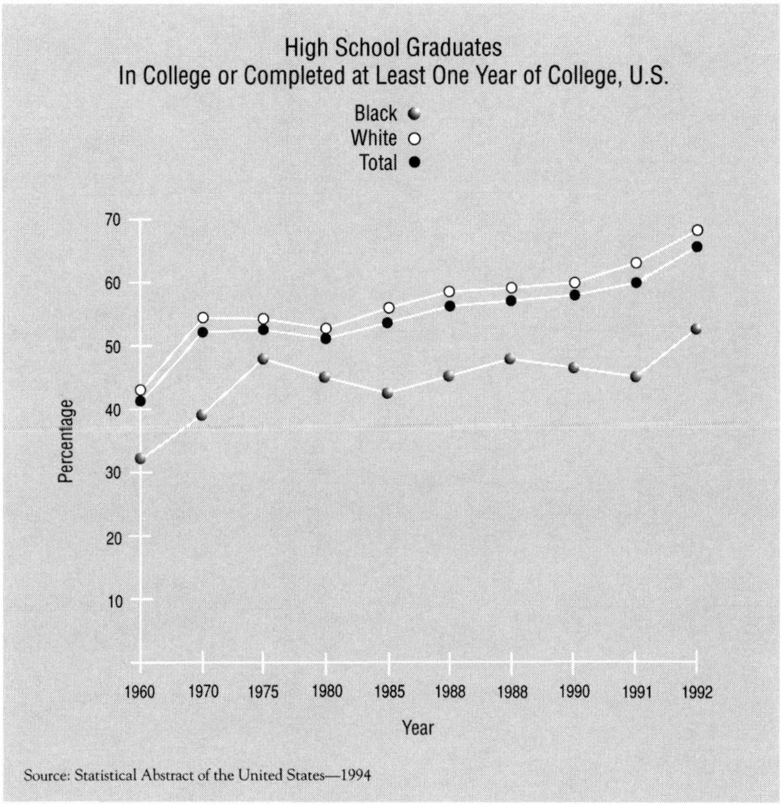

Figure 5.3

Another aspect of graduation to look at is how many people are graduating from college. This is a good indication of how well we are preparing ourselves for our new "third wave" communication-based society. Figure 5-4 shows the percentages of our population that have graduated from college. The percentage of whites graduating from college has increased from 8 percent in 1960 to 22 percent in 1993, and the percentage of blacks has increased from 3 percent in 1960 to 11 percent in 1993. These are increases of 175 percent for whites and 267 percent for blacks.

Again, this does not paint a picture of a broken education system. On the contrary, it shows a system that is continually meeting higher standards.

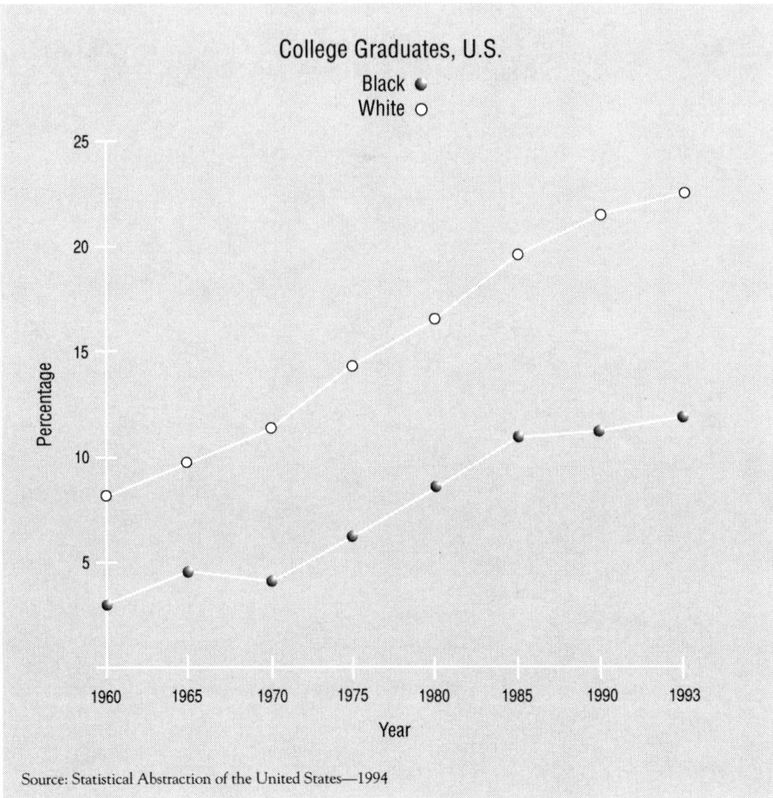

Figure 5.4

If we break down college attendance, we see more dramatic changes. Figure 5-5 shows the number of people by gender attending college since 1970. While it shows dramatic increases in both male and female enrollment, the most interesting feature is that significantly more females than males now attend college in the United States. This dramatic social change shows the new role of women in our modern society. Certainly, in educational opportunity, females have reached parity with males. (This fact also supports the discussion in Chapter 4 on population, as these women who are attending college will likely decide to have fewer children and to have them later in life.) The numbers are dramatic. Female enrollment has increased from 1.2 million in 1960 to 7.8 million in 1992, an increase of 550 percent. Male enrollment has increased from 2.3 million in 1960 to 6.1 million in 1992, an increase of 165 percent.

This reflects a wonderful increase in opportunity for women in our population and probably means as much for the future of our society as anything in this discussion. We are now beginning to use the brain power of all of our society, not just that of men.

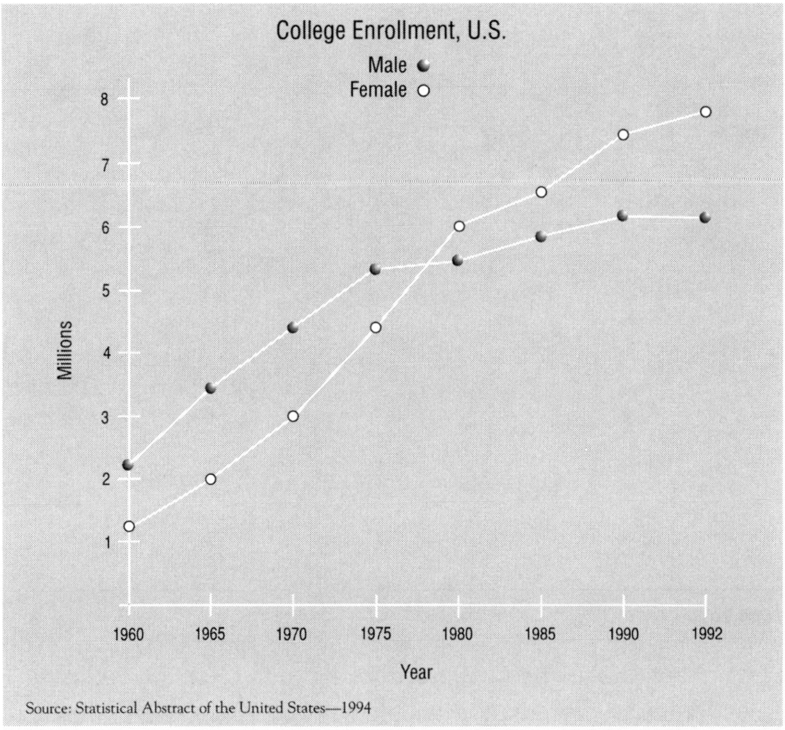

Figure 5.5

Another dramatic set of facts that illustrate the strength of our education system can be seen in Figure 5-6. It shows how our country's education compares with several of our major competing countries. The chart includes substantial data, but it simply shows that the United States, along with Canada, has the highest percentage of people with college degrees and has the lowest percentage of people who do not have at least a high school diploma. Eighty-three percent of people in the United States have completed high school or college and only 17

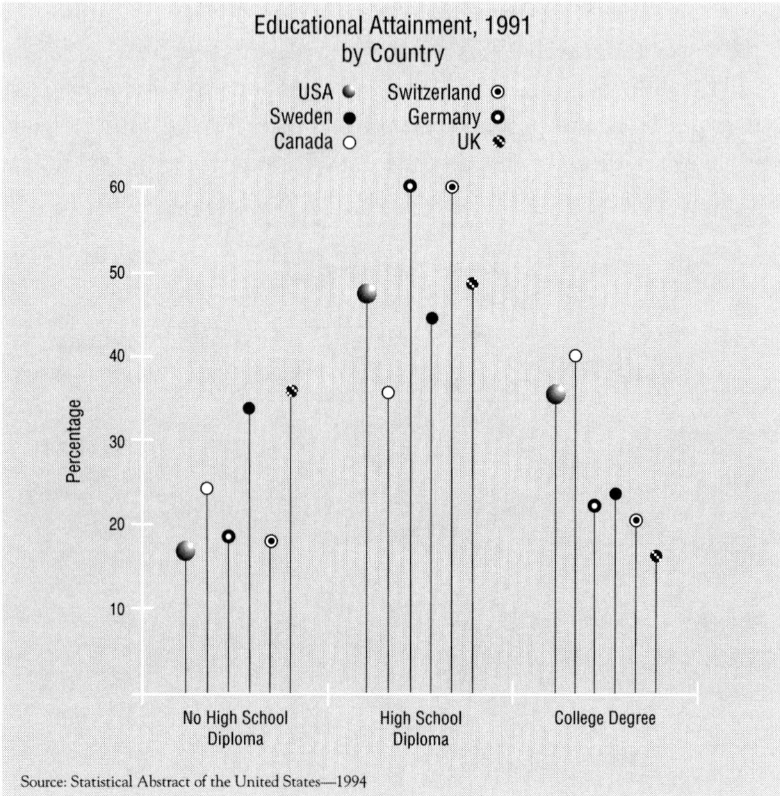

Figure 5.6

percent have not earned a high school diploma. Germany is closest to us with only 18 percent of its people without a high school diploma. Thirty-six percent of people in the United States have college degrees compared with twenty-two percent in Germany. The basic point of this chart is that the United States is doing the best job of any country in educating its people to the high levels the modern world demands.

Despite these facts about our education system, many people are still troubled feeling that our schools just aren't educating our children as well as they used to. We hear that our kids are doing worse and that their test scores keep decreasing. Well, what are the facts?

Figures 5-7 and 5-8 show that the average Scholastic Aptitude Test scores for both males and females have indeed dropped over the past twenty-five years. Average scores decreased during the period

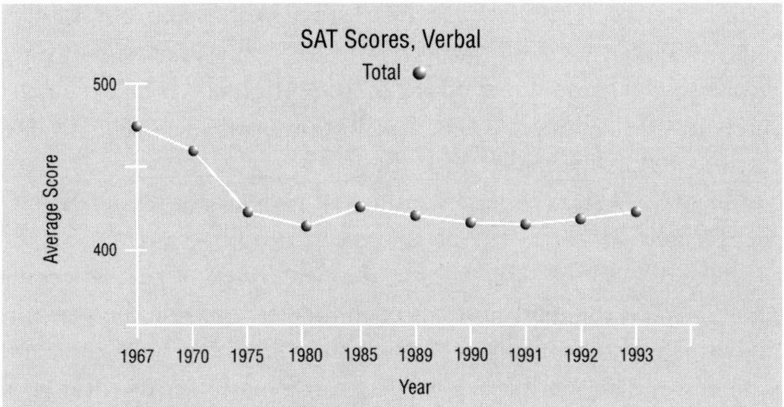

Source: Statistical Abstract of the United States—1994

Figure 5.7

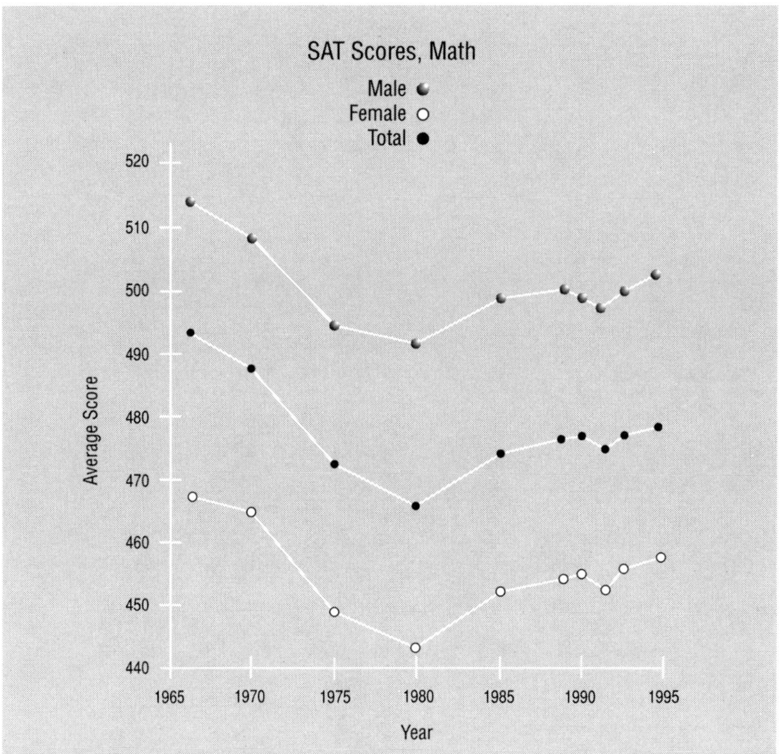

Source: Statistical Abstract of the United States—1994

Figure 5.8

from 1965 through 1980 and have stayed somewhat constant or improved slightly since 1980. The charts also show that females have always scored below males on the math portion of the SAT. Females scored above males on the verbal portion until the early '70s, but have scored below males since then.

Figure 5-9 shows the percentage of people scoring above 600, and Figure 5-10 shows the percentage of people scoring below 400 on the SAT. As the figures show, the percentage of people scoring above 600 on the math test has been increasing while the percentage of people scoring above 600 on the verbal has been constant. The percentage scoring below 400 on the math test has also been slightly increasing while it has been constant for the verbal test.

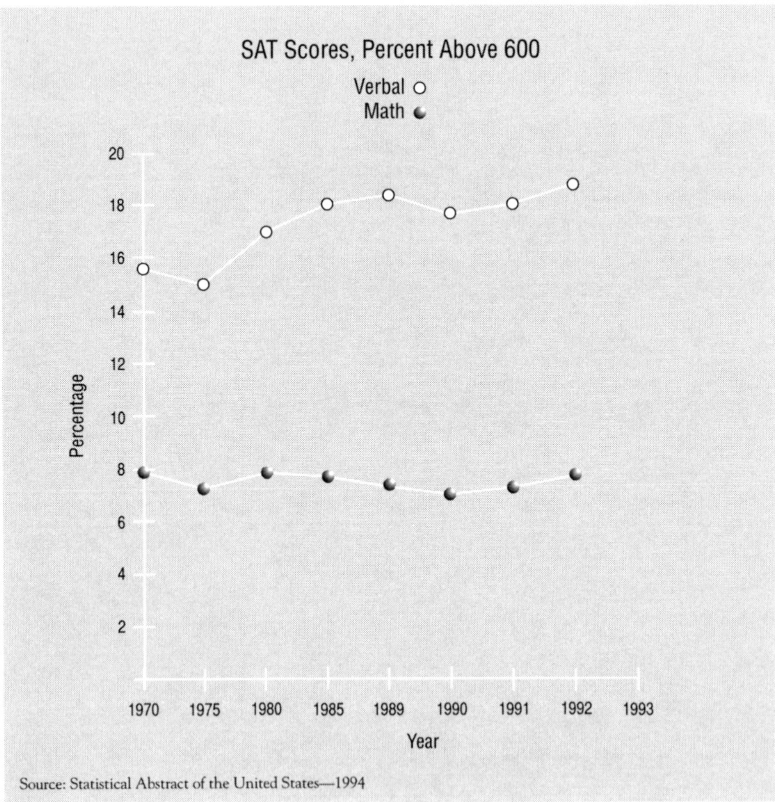

Figure 5.9

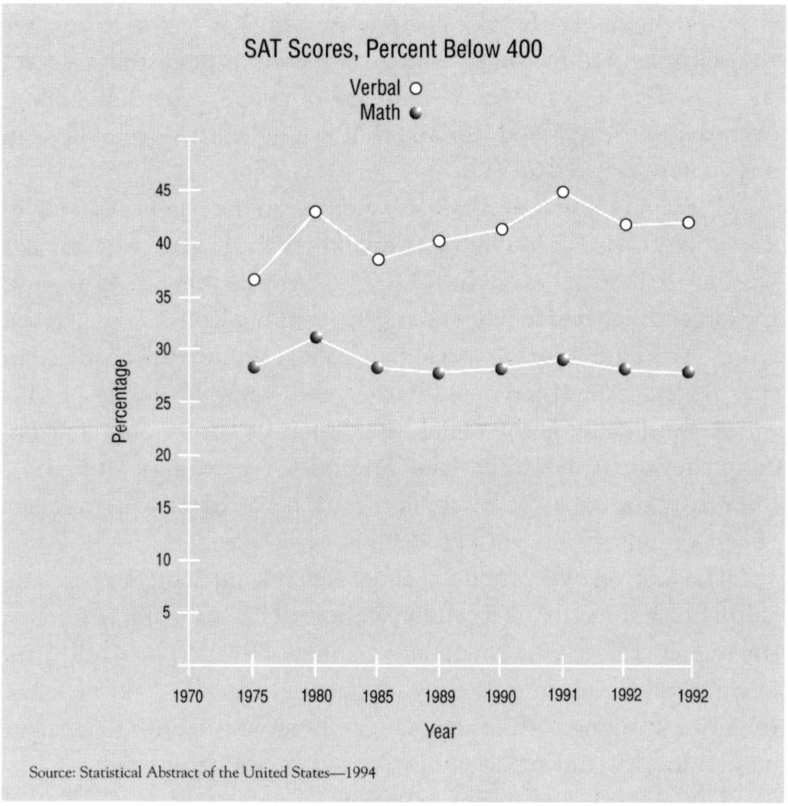

Figure 5.10

The fact that the percentage of people scoring above 600 on the math test is increasing is interesting. This might show that people aren't really doing worse on the SAT; the changes are primarily due to the changing demographics of the people taking the tests. There are more people, females, and minorities taking the tests than ever before, and this drove down the scores between 1960 and 1980. Since then, the makeup of the people taking the tests hasn't changed as much, and the scores have stayed fairly constant.

There is no question that the scores have dropped, but why have they dropped? The reasons are not simple.

One cause might be related to the much larger population base that is taking the tests. Since more people are attending college, there are more people taking the tests. This has served to remove the self selection factor, in which only college prep students take the test. The big changes in numbers of people attending college occurred in the '60s and '70s and that was when the biggest drop in test scores occurred as well.

A second cause is the dramatic increase in the number of females attending college. Although we don't know the reasons why females score lower than males on the SAT, it is a fact that they do. As a result, the larger number of females taking the tests has lowered the average scores. The largest increase in female college attendance occurred in the '60s and '70s, which was also when the average scores dropped.

A third cause is the racial integration of our schools that occurred during the last forty years. This cause is more difficult to show than the previous two. Forced integration has had two significant effects on our society, and probably on our test scores.

The first, and very positive, effect is that a much higher percentage of black students are attending college. This is a major reason for the higher college enrollment and graduation rates. The whole idea of integration was to give equal opportunity to all of our citizens. Integration, along with other changes in our society, has resulted in more minority students attending and graduating from college.

The second, and negative, effect of integration is the loss of "neighborhood" schools as children are bussed to other schools to achieve racial balance. The loss of a strongly focused neighborhood school removes parents from the same level of control and influence on schools and their programs. This may be the worst unforeseen result of integration.

Two nagging concerns about our schools remain and need to be discussed. First, we feel that our children just aren't learning as much, or at least the same things, as we did. Second, we think that violence in our schools has increased dramatically.

Even though the SAT scores don't completely support the concern that our children aren't learning as much earlier generations, we still are concerned that they aren't. When our kids can't spell, don't know basic geography, and can't put a sentence together, these are symptoms that tell us our children aren't learning as much as we did—or at least the same things or the same ways we learned.

Education today is certainly different. There is much less rote memorization. There are more attempts to teach understanding of principles rather than just memorization. Businesses demand "creative" employees who can think instead of simply list facts. There also is much more to teach: We now have computers, we need to teach other languages, and we must teach about AIDS and other social issues. All of these factors have affected the way teaching is done.

We also have to deal with integration. Kids are spending more time on buses, are going to schools outside their own neighborhoods, and must deal with drugs and crime wherever they go to school (see Chapter 6). These certainly affect their ability to study.

Another big change is in the family. There are more families in which both parents work. The result is that fewer parents have the time to work with schools and often parents are too tired or too busy to supervise their children's homework.

The nature of the teaching workforce has also changed. Teaching unions have become very powerful, often exercising effective control over the education system. These unions, as with all unions, work for their members. That means pushing for more pay for less work, which translates into active political lobbying for more money for schools. As a result, teaching has become a more financially attractive profession. The wages are now often competitive with other professions, and as a result, many schools are having difficulties making financial ends meet.

These effects on our schools have left the strong impression that our children aren't learning like they should be, or as well as the previous generations did. This might or might not be true. The figures on the number of people attending college don't support it, but SAT scores do support it. True or not, many of us believe it and we should treat our perception seriously.

Another obvious problem is the amount of crime and drugs in our schools. Although overall crime is decreasing in the United States, violent crime among young people has increased and is at its highest level ever (see Chapter 6 on crime).

Crime in our schools is a very disturbing problem, one for which there is no simple solution. The fundamental cause of crime is the lack of real hope for many of our young people as they face their futures.

As discussed earlier, a positive aspect of the U.S. education system is the large number of people who now attend college. While good news for our country and for those people fortunate enough to attend college, it does not help those people who do not or cannot attend.

Our society has entered a new revolution: the "third wave," the "information society," or whatever we choose to call it. This "new world" is one where people must be literate and educated if they are going to succeed. If they are not educated, they will not have the opportunities that were available to them in the past. Kids realize this.

So what should young people do? If they feel that they have no hope, they might become more likely to use drugs. This creates a ready market for others to move into to supply those drugs. Also, if they have no hope, there is less reason to obey societal rules, so they take out their frustrations through violence (see Chapter 6 on crime). This crime in schools isn't the schools' fault, but they must deal with it. And that takes time and energy away from teaching.

So, what does all of this mean and what should we do about it? This all tells us mainly that our schools are doing a better job than we think they are. They are graduating more students and sending more of them on to college. They are sending more females and minorities to college. And, SAT scores are not longer declining.

But things aren't perfect and major improvements are needed. Things we should be working on to improve our education system include the following:

- We should reconsider bussing, and consider restoring neighborhood schools
- We should reinstate teaching of memorization to help our kids learn those things that can only be memorized. For example, multiplication tables and spelling can be learned only through memorization and are necessary skills for living in our modern society.
- We should let our schools concentrate on teaching and stop assuming they can or should solve social problems.
- We must work harder to keep kids in school, particularly in the inner cities.

- Parents need to become and stay involved in their local schools.
- We need to work in our communities to solve the drug and crime problems.

These problems and solutions aren't new. They are well known and receive much attention by politicians and the press. What is often ignored, though, is the fact that schools really are doing a good job. An improvement that is still needed is to involve the children not currently reached by the education system, although that percentage of the population is the smallest it has ever been.

6

Crime

THE CONVENTIONAL WISDOM IS THAT CRIME is constantly getting worse in the United States and, indeed, in much of the Western world. The facts show, however, that the situation is more complex than that. While overall crime has not changed much over the last twenty years, the rate of violent crime has increased. Figure 6-1 shows the overall crime index in the United States for the last twenty years. A careful look at the graph shows that the crime rate has stayed around 5,600 per 100,000 people for most of that period. The graph's fluctuations show that the rate increased rapidly between 1974 and 1980, dropped until 1984, increased again until 1991, and then started decreasing once again.

The property crime index for the same period can be seen in Figure 6-2. This index shows little change over the twenty-year period, peaking in 1980 and generally declining since then. The rapid buildup from 1974 to 1980 is worth noting.

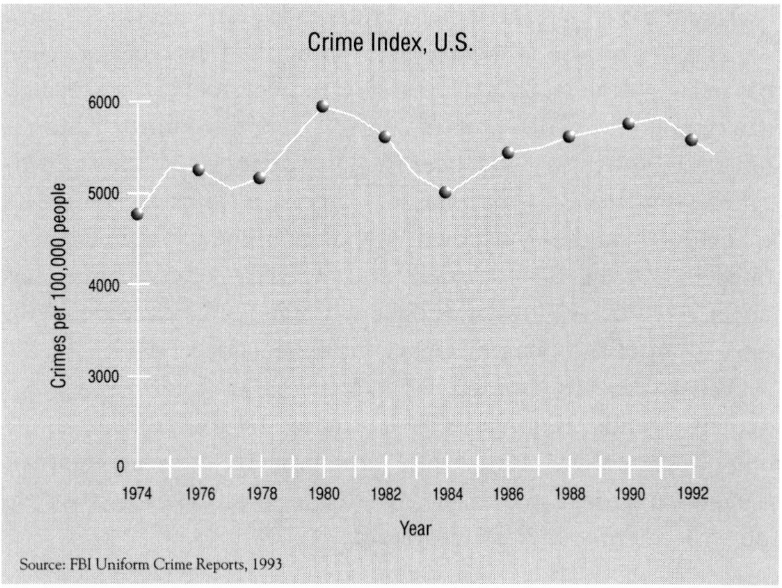

Figure 6.1

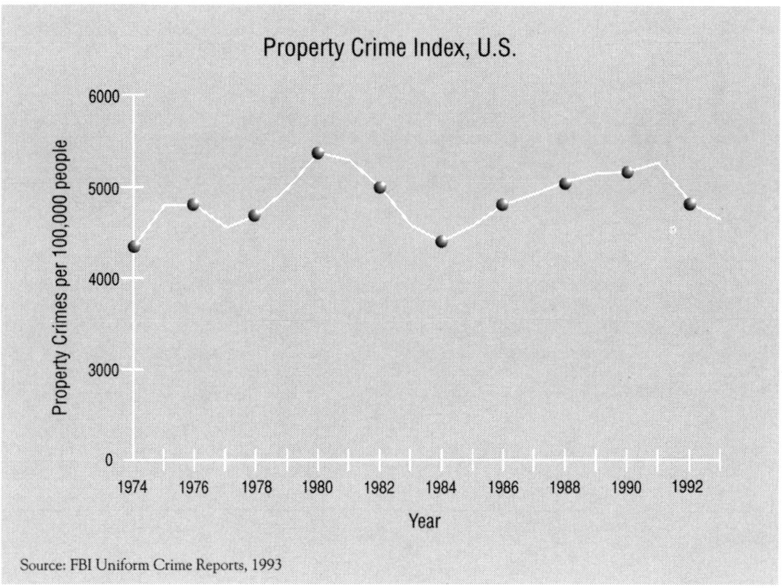

Figure 6.2

Figure 6-3 shows the violent crime index and Figures 6-5, 6-6, 6-7, and 6-8 on the following pages show the four types of crime that make up the violent crime index: murder, robbery, aggravated assault, and rape. This series of charts is very disturbing because it shows the growth in crime over the last twenty years. This growth is the reason crime has become such a great issue for all of us. The five charts show that the growth in violent crime has been concentrated in the aggravated assault and rape categories. Murder has shown very little change and robbery has had only modest growth. Rates in all of the categories have decreased since 1991.

What does this data tell us?

The overall crime index is dominated by the property crime index because there are so many more property crimes committed than violent crimes. We should therefore look at the property crime and violent crime indices separately.

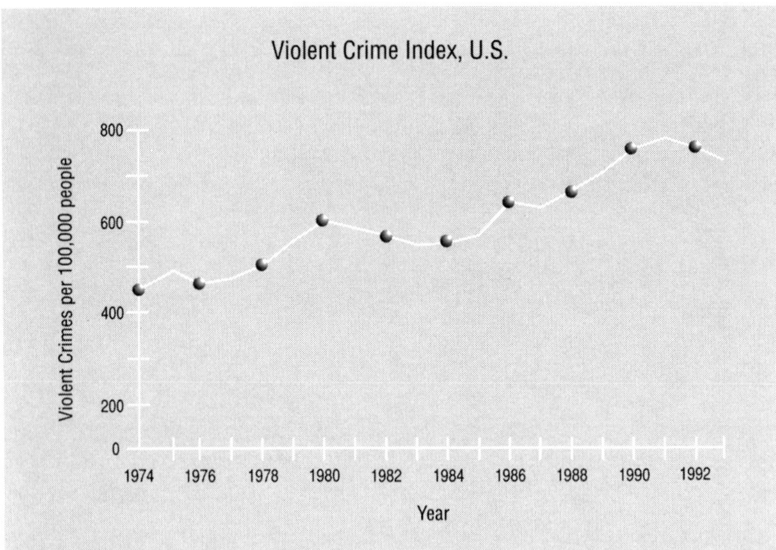

Source: FBI Uniform Crime Reports—1993

Figure 6.3

Property Crime

The property crime index steadily increased in the late '70s, dropped during the early '80s, increased again in the late '80s, and has been decreasing in the early '90s. The index peaked in 1980 and has generally shown a downward trend since then. Its 1993 value of 4,737 is 11.5 percent below the peak value of 5,353.

Why was it highest in 1980 and why would it have declined since then? My research has uncovered little to explain the trend. This might be because the conventional wisdom is that the problem is bad and only getting worse, and little study has been done on why the rates are improving now.

However, I do have an opinion on the reasons for the trends. The early increase is most likely due to the gradual deterioration of the traditional family in the United States coupled with the breakdown of societal restraints traditionally used to control individuals.

Young people commit most of the crimes in any society, and young people in the United States in the late '70s were struggling with new challenges as our country changed. Most people who commit crimes are between fifteen and twenty-five years old, which means that a fifteen-year old in 1975 would have been born and raised in the '60s. That was a difficult time for all of us, and was an especially difficult time for young people. I believe that this age group was more rebellious than normal teenagers, and this is reflected in the crime rates for that period.

The country was also going through difficult economic times in the late '70s. We were encountering the energy crisis, were in a recession with high inflation (stagflation), and were still very concerned about the nuclear threat from the USSR. These situations probably contributed to the unrest among the young and to the resulting crime.

After 1980, societal conditions stabilized and the crime rate declined. This was most likely due to the changing demographics in the United States. Because of the decline in the birth rate, fewer teenagers were coming into the fifteen to twenty-five year old bracket.

After 1984, things began to worsen again. No large demographic trends can explain these changes, but they might reflect the growth of inner city gang problems and of related drug problems.

After 1990, crime rates started to improve again. While it is too early to tell, the most likely reasons are that the courts are now using stiffer penalties and our society is concentrating more of its attention on crime. Crime has become the number one issue in America and authorities are responding to that concern. It is possible that the reduction in crime over the last three years is mostly due to the fact that more criminals are in prison, preventing them from committing any additional crimes. Figure 6-4 shows the dramatic increase in prisoners in our prisons over the last twenty years.

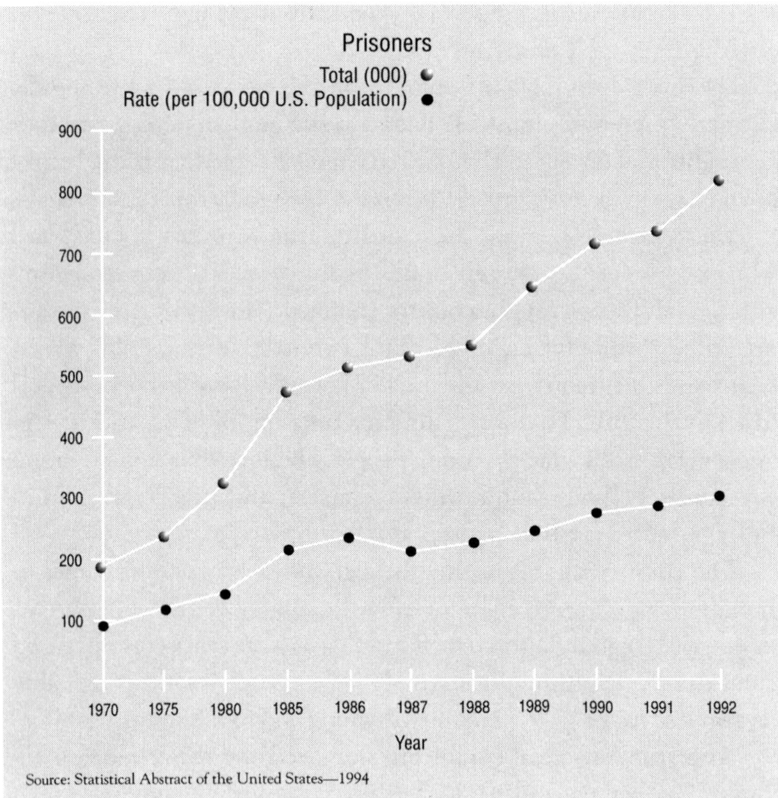

Figure 6.4

To summarize, crimes against property haven't changed significantly over the last twenty years. This is opposite to the general feeling most of us have that all crime is getting worse. Property crime clearly is not.

Violent Crime

As opposed to property crime, violent crime has been getting worse for most of the last twenty years. From an index of 461 in 1974, it climbed fairly steadily to 758 in 1991 before falling slightly in 1992 and 1993. That is an increase between 1974 and 1991 of 64.4 percent! As I mentioned earlier, much of the increase is concentrated in the aggravated assault and rape categories, which grew by 104.6 percent and 101.5 percent, respectively, during the same period. Robbery grew by a more modest 30.6 percent. Murder, on the other hand, has declined by 3.2 percent. Why would assault and rape show such a large increase when property crime and murder show only modest increases or show declines?

Source: FBI Uniform Crime Reports—1993

Figure 6.5

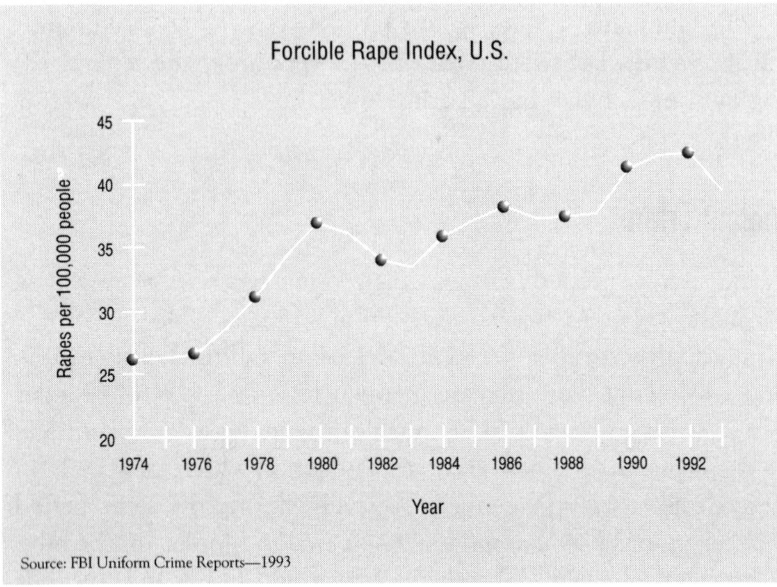

Figure 6.6

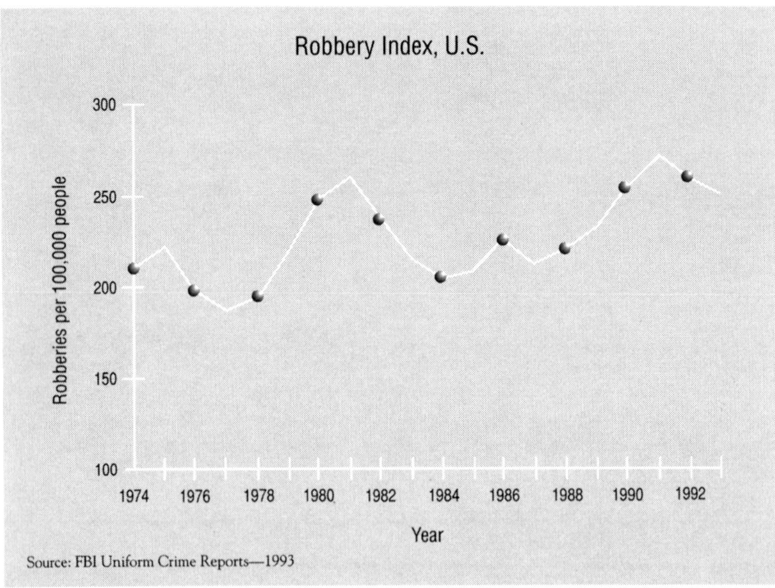

Figure 6.7

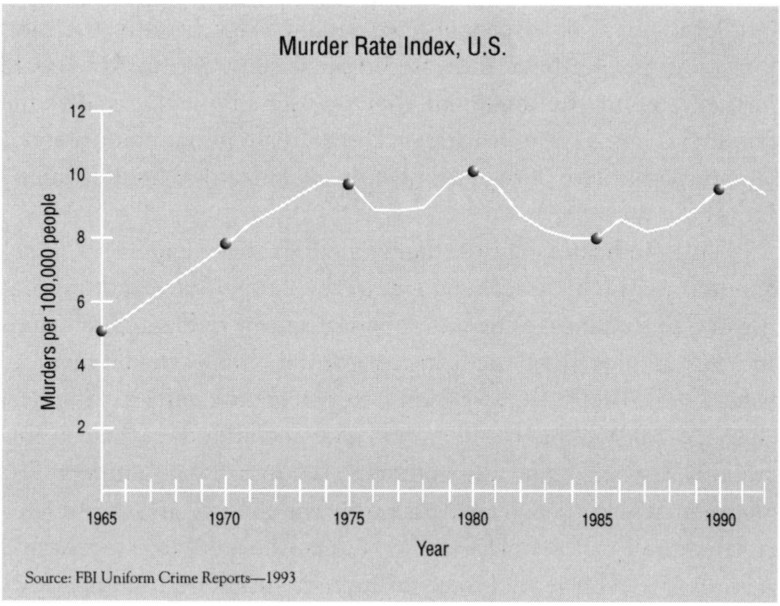

Figure 6.8

The breakdown of the traditional family in America is probably a major contributor to the changes in crime rates, particularly for violent crimes. The nature of the worst two categories, aggravated assault and rape, are that they are crimes against people, most likely against people that are known by or are in proximity to the perpetrator. These are crimes of passion and power committed by people who, for some reason, are out of control.

These people might be out of control because of drug or alcohol abuse. They might be out of control because of gang or peer pressure. They might be angry with society because they feel left out or feel they do not have a chance in the modern world. They might be out of control because of a relationship problem. All of these reasons suggest some consideration of a lack of early guidance that a stable family life could have provided.

The murder rates offer further insight to support to this discussion. As mentioned earlier, murder has actually declined slightly over the last twenty years, particularly during the last three years. But this doesn't hold true when we look at rates for young people. While murder rates for older people have declined significantly, the rates for young people have increased dramatically. Again, this could further support the argument that the decline of the traditional family has had a great bearing on the increase in our country's violent crime because of the lack of early guidance that a stable family life would provide.

Other indicators of the changing nature of violent crime in our country are the historical changes in the murder rates and the timing of those changes. The murder chart shown in Figure 6-8 begins in 1965. Its most dramatic feature is the doubling of the murder rate from 1965 to 1975, corresponding to two great events in America: the Vietnam War and the liberation movement. Both of these events could be considered as contributors to the increase in murders. The Vietnam War caused great division in our country and an increase in the number of people who lost respect for our government and institutions. The results were an increase in alternative lifestyles, resisting authority and use of drugs. It appears that the increase in murder rates followed these changes. Although the liberation movement had the positive effect of freeing women in our society to have more control over their lives, it also contributed to the breakup of the traditional family.

These violent crime and murder trends are both disturbing and enlightening. They are disturbing because we don't want to see them. None of us want to see our country become increasingly dangerous and to have our children grow up in a society where there is constant fear of crime. On the other hand, these trends can be enlightening if we can understand what they are telling us.

To understand crime, we must understand the people who commit crimes. Crime and incarceration statistics show that most crimes are committed by young people—in particular by young males. Much of the crime is committed by young black males. What is it that makes these young people commit crimes?

First, they have a lack of control. We all know that is true. We all have been teenagers and most of us have been around teenagers or have raised teenagers. Teenagers go through a period of great difficulty as they struggle through the transition from childhood to adulthood. People at this age need a lot of help. This help, or guidance, was traditionally given by the family and supported by the village. The African proverb, "it takes a whole village to raise a child," is very true.

Second, they might have a real problem with how fast our society is changing and the difficulties that this presents. Jobs for uneducated people aren't as available as they used to be. People who might not be properly prepared for the information age justifiably feel that there is no hope for them.

Third, they might have been raised in a home environment without a positive male role model, and have never been shown how they should behave as responsible male members of our society.

Fourth, they might have been abused as a child. It is well known that this is devastating to a child, and that a very high percentage of felons were abused when they were young.

And, fifth, they probably are abusing drugs or alcohol or both. This abuse might be related to some of the above items.

What can or should be done about the violent crime problem? We are already doing much of what should be done. We have stiffened sentences and are jailing more felons for longer periods. We have new laws, such as "three strikes and you are out," to put repeat offenders into prison for life. But these solutions do not address the deeper problem of the breakdown of the family.

Our society is finally beginning to recognize that changes in the family structure, and in particular the absence of fathers from the family environment, is one of the major causes of the high violent crime rate in the United States. In fact, it may be the major cause!

We are also recognizing alcoholism and the other problems it causes, and are becoming more able to bring it out into the open and treat the problem itself. We are also becoming more open about child abuse. We are all very disturbed by this topic, but at least we are discussing it. These are all good steps in beginning to solve these problems, but we must do more to ensure lasting solutions.

We also need to change the incentives and acceptances in our society to encourage families to stay together. Single parenthood is a very difficult task under any circumstances, no matter what the reason. We should do all we can to help people avoid the problems that they will have as single parents. Divorce should be discouraged whenever possible. Fathers should be encouraged to be with and stay with their children. While we love all children, we should encourage their birth into two parent families. And, when people are left as single parents, we should give them the training they need to successfully raise their children, particularly through the teen years.

When I started to write this chapter, I knew that the crime rate was coming down in America. I also knew that the murder rate was coming down. I thought I would be able to point out these facts and show that crime is decreasing in America even though we all think it is getting worse. I found out that it isn't that simple. While overall crime and murder may be decreasing, other types of violent crime have only just started to decline, and it is way too early to call these trends.

However, I do think that this review shows that we need to return to two-parent families in America, and that if we can do that, we will be pleased with the results. Many other things we are doing are having positive effects and are reducing crime rates, even with the problem of the breakdown of the nuclear family. If we can keep up those programs and, at the same time, put our families back together, we will go a long way towards solving the crime problem.

7

Balance of Payments

THE CONVENTIONAL WISDOM CONSISTENTLY REPORTED in the news wrings its hands over the United States' persistent negative balance of payments. Our negative balance of payments has persisted for several years, and we are constantly being told that it is a bad thing and is making the United States a second-class country. We have become afraid of Japan, and our government seems to believe that one of its major tasks is to criticize Japan's trade policies.

With all of this concern, and with the persistence of the negative balance for fifteen years, why has the United States remained so strong and why has it clearly regained—in fact, expanded—the lead as the most productive country in the world? (See Chapter 8 on productivity.)

The basic reason is that it is not bad to have a negative balance of payments. In fact, it can be argued that it is actually good for a country. Currently, three of the countries with the largest negative balance of payments are Korea, Malaysia, and Thailand, which also happen to be three of the fastest growing countries in the world. All three are part of the Asian revolution, in which Asia is emerging as the most dynamic growth region in the world.

Another interesting fact is that the two countries that historically had among the largest negative balance of payments are the two that have the strongest economies in the world today: the United States and Japan.

The United States had the highest negative balance in history (when measured against the total Gross National Product) during the late nineteenth century. That was the time period when we experienced our most dramatic growth. We became a major economic power in the world, explored and developed the West, built railroads across the country, built a steel industry, began to be build automobiles, and developed many other parts of our modern industrial society. Of course, we couldn't afford to pay for all of this growth ourselves. Money, or capital, had to be brought into the country to pay for all of it. And that money created a negative balance of payments.

Japan had the highest negative balance of payments for the twenty years or so after the end of World War II. It was during that time that they rebuilt their country after its devastation during the war. As with the United States, they couldn't pay for it all themselves, so they had to import capital. This capital enabled them to build a very strong economy to put them in the competitive position that they are in today.

So what about the United States today? Figure 7-1 shows our recent history of imports, exports, and merchandise trade balance. It shows some very interesting trends. Our imports have shown a nice steady growth over the twenty-five-year period shown, growing from about $40 billion annually in 1970 to about $600 billion in 1993. At the same time, our exports have grown from about $45 billion in 1970 to about $450 billion in 1993. We now do the most trade of any country in the world; we are number one in both imports and exports.

The chart clearly shows what has happened to our negative balance of payments. The account was significantly negative in the early '80s. This was caused by a pause in the growth of exports while imports continued to grow. Since then, exports have continued to grow parallel with imports, keeping the balance of payments somewhat constant at about $140 billion annually. An understanding of what happened in the early '80s might help us understand the real effects of a negative balance of payments.

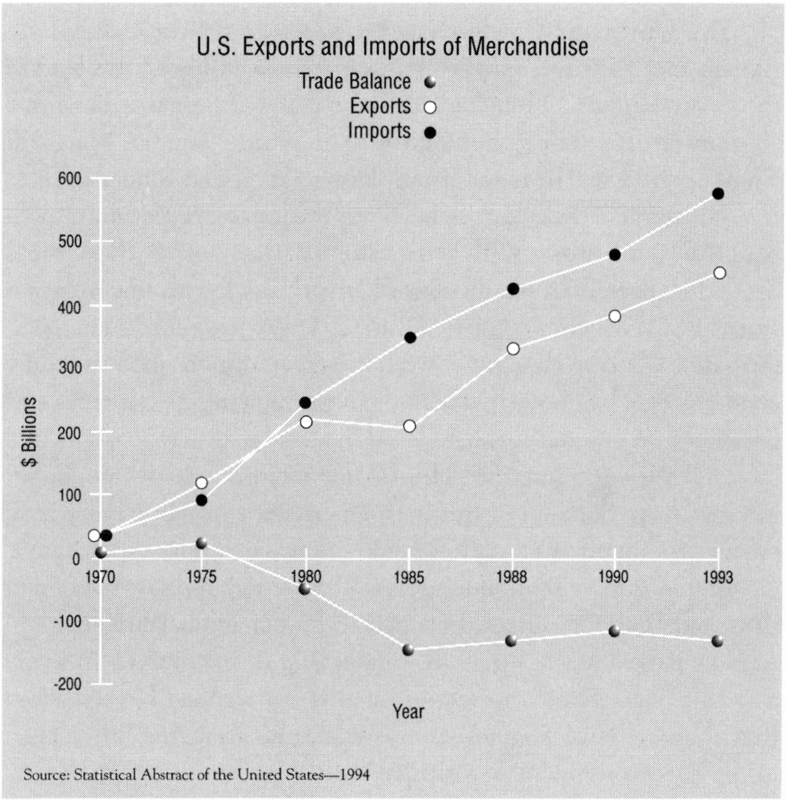

Figure 7.1

As we all know, the early '80s corresponded to the early years of the Reagan Presidency. That period represented a major shift in the economic policies of the United States and, indeed, of the world. Whether it is called Reaganomics, supply-side economics, trickle-down economics, or the conservative revolution, it represented a profound change in thinking about what works and what doesn't work in economic systems.

The fundamental change was the realization that socialism and increasing government controls over the economy weren't working, and that giving the private sector more opportunities was the key to economic growth. In a sense, it can be said that Adam Smith defeated Karl Marx.

The United States clearly led the world in these changes, although many other countries participated or followed the lead of the United States. Other countries who adopted similar policies had similar results. They included Great Britain (under Margaret Thatcher), Japan, Korea, Taiwan, Hong Kong, and Singapore.

The result of these U.S. policies was the longest peacetime growth period in our history. With only a short pause in 1990, the United States has been on a steady upward growth track with low inflation since 1982. No other country in history has experienced such a performance. During that time, we have created more jobs than any economy ever has, have reinvented our manufacturing industries (see Chapter 8 on productivity), have led the information revolution, and have led the world into the "Third Wave" of industrial development. And we have done all of this with a persistent negative balance of payments that many predicted would surely damage us. But it hasn't.

In addition to economic success, this period also saw the end of the Cold War. Countries that used to be our implacable enemies, such as Russia and China, are now trying to emulate us in every way they can. The basic reason for this is that they have realized that their socialist systems do not work and that they have been losing the economic war with the West.

But what did economic performance have to do with the balance of payments?

During the early '80s, the United States was experiencing strong economic growth that was stimulated by the early features of Reagan's programs, particularly the tax cuts and the reduction in regulations. Similar growth did not occur elsewhere in the rest of the world because the other major trading countries had not yet made the changes necessary to stimulate such growth.

As a result of this difference in economic performance, the U.S. economy required more goods and services proportionally than did the rest of the world. This meant that we imported more from other countries than they needed to buy from us. Imports continued their steady growth while exports slowed down. Once other countries began to adopt policies similar to those in the United States, they started growing again and our exports began to increase.

What has happened, though, is that the rest of the world has never caught up with the U.S. growth rate. While we have experienced steady growth, most of the rest of the world has stumbled into periodic recessions. This scenario occurred most dramatically in our three largest trading partners: Canada, Mexico, and Japan. Slowdowns in their growth rates have limited their purchases from us, causing our exports to lag behind our imports. When those three countries get their economies back on track, we can be fairly assured that our balance of payments will start to come back into balance.

There is another, very important, way to look at balance of payments. That is to look at the whole picture which includes the flow of the money necessary to pay for the negative balance. You can be sure that the money accounts are in balance, which means that people in other countries have been willing to send us money to fund the negative balance, dollar for dollar.

In our current world economy, the amount of money that is transferred through the international money markets on a daily basis is almost unbelievable. On the Eurodollar exchange at Chicago's Mercantile Exchange, there is over $4 trillion in play every day. That is as much money as is reflected in the entire U.S. economy for a year. Our $150 billion trade deficit represents only 3.75 percent of the amount of money available to be traded daily on a single exchange.

The point of the above is that the trade deficit, even though it is very large, seems fairly small when compared with the size of the world economy and with the flow of money around the world.

Another way to look at the money flowing into the United Stated to fund the negative trade balance is to look at it as an investment. People who have sent that money (remember it has been dollar for dollar to fund the gap in imports and exports) have felt that it was a good place to invest their money. They have been investing in America. They wouldn't have sent their money if they didn't think it was a good investment.

When viewed from other countries, the United States is a very desirable place to invest. It is the world's largest economy and market, and is stable. Its currency is holding its value and is the common currency used around the world. It is the most productive country in the world, is the world's largest trading country, and is experiencing steady non-inflationary growth. In total, it is a very good place to invest money.

And this is just what has been happening. People in other countries have been investing heavily in the United States. This investment money has been used to help fund the steady and strong growth that we have been enjoying for the last fourteen years.

To summarize, a negative balance of payments in an economy as strong as the United States is more of a good thing than a bad thing. This is particularly true currently for the United States, with a non-inflationary economy and a solid, stable currency. That has been the case in the United States over the last fourteen years. The money that has come in to fund the negative balance of payments has been used to help fund the economic growth that we have had over that period. Without that funding, our growth would not have been as strong.

The one valid concern that people have is that foreigners are owning more and more of America. While this might be disturbing to some people, it isn't necessarily a bad thing. We didn't think it was such a bad thing when we invested all over the world in the years following World War II. In fact, we probably should be flattered that so many people around the world want to invest here.

So, contrary to conventional wisdom, the negative balance of payments of the United States over the last fourteen years has been a positive thing for our country. During this time, we have had the longest and most successful peacetime growth period that any country has had ever. While the balance of payments is not the primary cause of these successes, it is a result of the successes. Our economic growth has been dramatic and has outstripped growth in the rest of the world. As a result, we are importing more than we are exporting, resulting in a negative balance of payments. Because of the nature of our country and our economy, the rest of the world has been willing to invest here to fund the balance of payments and to fund our continued growth.

Altogether, a very good deal—especially for the United States!

8

Productivity

THE CONVENTIONAL WISDOM AND PREVAILING OPINION in the United States ever since the oil crisis in the '70s is that our productivity is poor compared to what it was historically, and compared to other countries. We also believe it is getting worse. We have become especially paranoid about Japan in this regard and now tend to believe that Japan is more productive than us and that we can't possibly compete with them.

Nothing could be further from the truth. America is and always has been the most productive nation in the world.

As with many of the other subjects in this book, productivity has not been covered well or accurately by the press. Ever since the United States lost some of its confidence in the Vietnam War and the ensuing energy crisis of the late '60s and early '70s, the press and many politicians have continually criticized our country over the "problem." One of their popular laments was to claim the loss of our productivity lead, particularly when compared to Japan.

People used statistics over and over again to show that Japan was more productive than we were. How could this be true when just a few short years before, they had been recovering from World War II and were known for producing shoddy goods?

First of all, the claims were simply not true. Japan is not and never was more productive than the United States. Figure 8-1 shows the per capita gross domestic product of several countries for the last twenty years. This particular figure adjusts for purchasing power differences between the countries. Note that the United States has always been at the top with Switzerland coming in a close second. Our major competitors in the world economy, Germany and Japan, are behind us in productivity and have been for the entire period. As I said above, the United States is and always has been the most productive country in the world.

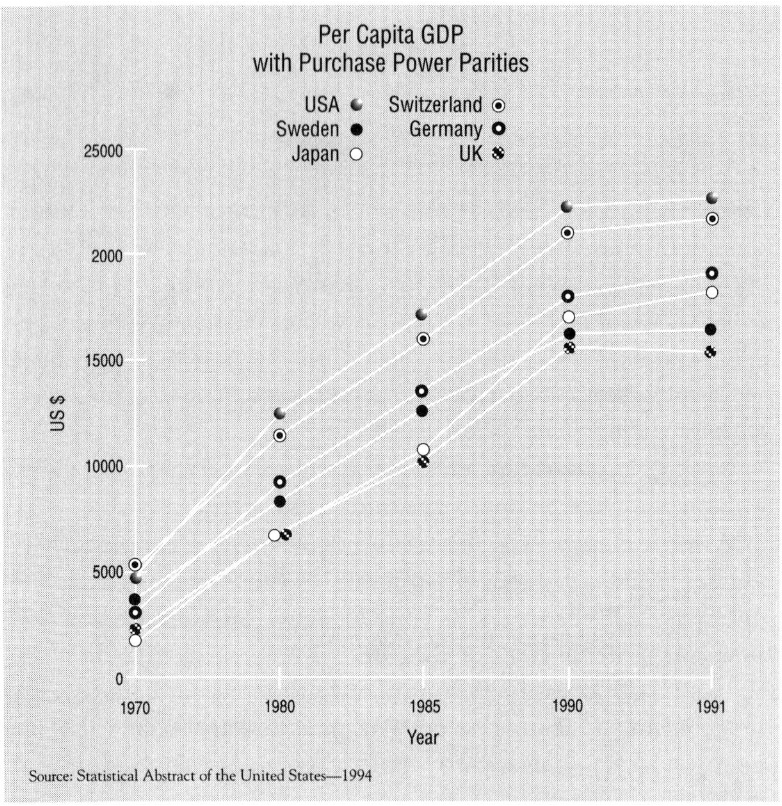

Figure 8.1

The misinformation that the press and politicians promoted was based on using the statistic of productivity growth, or rate of change of productivity, as if it was absolute productivity. During much of the '70s and '80s, the United States did have a lower rate of productivity growth than did Japan or Germany. In fact, the United States currently has a lower level of productivity growth than many countries in the world.

It is important to understand the difference between measuring something and measuring the change in something over time. These two measures are not even close to being the same. For example, a person who runs a four-minute mile today and runs another four-minute mile next month has run two very fast miles, but has shown 0 percent improvement in performance between the two runs. On the other hand, a person could run a slow ten-minute mile today and then improve to a still slow eight-minute mile next month. He would still be only half as fast as the first runner, but would have improved his time by 20 percent. Even if he can never run as fast as the first runner, his rate of change in time is much better than the first runner.

Another example, more closely related to the economic theme of this book, is to consider two workers, one earning $100,000 per year and one earning $20,000. If the first worker was able to increase her earnings by 5 percent per year and the second was able to increase hers by 15 percent per year (three times as fast), the first worker would still increase her earnings by more total dollars than the second worker. The first worker would be increasing her earnings by $5000 per year and the second worker would be increasing hers by only $3000 per year. The percentage increase by the second worker is higher, but the absolute change in dollars is smaller.

The second example is very similar to what happens when productivity gains are compared around the world. Countries that have low initial levels of productivity can often make large productivity gains, thus showing a large change in productivity growth. This change can make it appear as if they are going to pass up the countries with higher productivity levels. However, it is easy to overlook the absolute lead of the most productive countries and that their modest gains actually represent more actual gain than in the developing countries.

Part of the good news on this subject is that less productive countries can do a lot of catching up. And, in fact, they have done exactly that. Although the United States is still the most productive country in the world, many countries are now close to us. Most of these countries have had to recover from wars and improve their political-economic situations to reach a condition where growth was possible. When both of these situations were under control, rapid growth became possible and they quickly closed the gap between themselves and the United States. Despite these gains by other countries, the United States continues to set the standard.

These rapidly changing countries include all of Western Europe (including Spain, Portugal, and Turkey); Japan and the four tigers of East Asia: South Korea, Taiwan, Hong Kong, and Singapore; Canada; and, to a lesser extent, Mexico.

Now, with the ending of the Cold War and the advent of more liberal democracies and capitalism in other countries, many parts of the world are now able to enjoy the fruits of increased productivity and the resulting increase in living standards. Eastern Europe, Russia, China, India, and most of South America are all having varying degrees of success in emulating the United States and installing some form of capitalist system to allow their economy to grow.

One of the major reasons that developing countries can improve their productivity so rapidly is because of their ability to buy technology from the more developed countries. Technology and its required capital investment is one of the primary ways that productivity is increased. It is well known that people running machines in a factory will be more productive than the same people trying to make things on their own. The technology exists in the world to make these improvements and, if the capital can be found to make investments in machinery, then developing countries can make a fairly rapid improvement in their productivity.

If the United States wants to continue to lead, then its job—and that of the rest of the developed world—must be to stay ahead in the development and application of new technologies and methods. We must continue to be the best in using our brain power and creativity so that we can continue to be the supplier of the newest technologies and methods to the rest of the world.

It is in this area where the United States has excelled, especially in that last ten years. For most of this century, the United States has taken the lead in the development of new science and in the application of new technologies and methods to the world economy. Starting with the inventions of Edison at the turn of the century and continuing with the invention or major application of such things as airplanes, nuclear power, transistors, computers, software, television, motion pictures, and genetically engineered products, the United States has led the world in the development of most of the technology that has made our modern civilization possible.

Several reasons exist for our leadership in this area. Our liberal democracy and insistence on maximum freedom for the individual are probably the main reasons. The United States provides the best rewards in the world for entrepreneurship and invention. Many people come here from other countries to participate in the opportunities that exist here. And, over the years, we have tended to welcome these people. One of the best examples is the emigration of Albert Einstein from Germany to America to escape the Nazis.

Another reason for our success in developing new technology is that we have been able to afford to encourage invention. The United States is a wealthy country and has the resources to enable people to spend the time necessary to develop and invent new things.

Several other chapters of this book discuss other reasons why the United States has been able to keep the lead in the development and application of technology. Our readily available energy, excellent transportation system, and welcoming of people from all over the world have contributed to our successes. But, perhaps most important has been our education system—in particular, our higher education system. We educate more people and educate them to a higher degree than any other country. The attractiveness of our colleges and universities to people from other parts of the world is the strongest testimony to that fact.

And finally, a higher percentage of our population is active in our economy than in any other country. While many people are frustrated and threatened by our civil rights and equality of opportunity laws, the fact remains that we now use far more of our female and minority populations in our economy than ever before. And we use more than any other country. The true liberal experiment in the world in the last century has been the United States.

This expansion of the brain pool to include all of our population can be seen in the charts used in the chapter on education. Figures 5-2 through 5-5 show some of the increases that have been made in the opportunities for females and minorities in the United States in the last fifty years. There is no question that the country is much stronger today because it is using the brain power of most of its population instead of just that of its majority (white male) population. Many other countries of the world, including Japan, still do not involve females or other minorities in the mainstream economic life of their societies.

Even though the United States never actually lost its productivity lead over the rest of the world, we believed that we had during the '70s and early '80s. Perhaps this was good because it stimulated us to more and better action to regain the lead we thought we had lost. Our focus on productivity growth instead of on productivity was one of the reasons we felt so strongly that we had to do something about our productivity.

The result was that we improved on our already strong position. In the 1994 edition of the World Competitiveness Report, prepared jointly by the Lausanne, Switzerland-based International Institute for Management Development and the Geneva, Switzerland-based World Economic Forum, the United States ranked first in the world in competitiveness. This report compares 44 economies on over 100 measures of economic strength and lists the United States in first place followed by Singapore, Japan, Hong Kong, and Germany. This is a major improvement over our performance on this measure in the recent past.

What did the United States do? I think we just decided that we were not going to be anything but first in the future. And we got busy. Although many of our industries have always been the world's leaders, they improved their position even more. This includes the computer, chemical, pharmaceutical, and the entertainment industries. Some of our industries that had gotten sloppy and were no longer competitive in the world market had to reinvent themselves. These included the automobile, steel, and microchip industries, which have gone through major changes in the last ten to twenty years and have emerged leaner and more competitive on the world economic stage.

Many new technologies and management principles have been applied to accomplish these improvements, including such things as corporate takeovers, junk bonds, down sizing, middle management layoffs, total quality management, just-in-time inventories, and other systems for productivity improvement. Some of these have been very threatening to the people involved. All of these changes share some common characteristics.

First, all of these changes are part of the information age or the communications revolution. Perhaps the application of the computer and our rapid communications have influenced the changes more than anything else. Most of these major improvements in productivity would not be possible without the computer and none would be possible without our educated workforce.

With the tools and educated workforce now available, many things that we now take for granted just wouldn't be possible. Fax machines, Federal Express, cellular telephones, laptop computers, and pagers are just a few of these things. Our current business—and in some cases, personal—lives now revolve around this technology, much of which didn't exist a few short years ago. It, along with all the other new technologies and methods, is contributing to the explosive growth in productivity that we are now experiencing.

It isn't without cost, however. As I said above, many people feel very threatened by these changes. Uneducated or illiterate people might feel especially intimidated. These changes all revolve around the "Third Wave" or Information Revolution. People no longer can go to work in steel mills and receive good wages. Those jobs are disappearing the same way that farm jobs disappeared fifty years ago. They are being replaced by machines and computers. And the machines and computers are being operated by literate people.

Another group that is threatened is the large cadre of "middle management." Again, with the major improvements in communication and with the increases in the education level of the workforce, there is not as much need for middle management in the traditional sense. Removing layers of management is a common method of improving productivity in the modern world.

As a result, people must get educated in order to prosper. They are having to learn to do new things. The information age is here and we are being required to go through the changes in our society to accommodate it. Programmers are replacing steel workers.

Fortunately, the United States has the society in the world that is—and always has been—the most receptive to change. When I define us as a liberal democracy, I mean that we are ready to try new things in an open and free society. We are free to succeed and are also free to fail. We are constantly tearing down things so they can be rebuilt. We do it with both physical things like buildings and we do it with systems and methods like total quality management. This constant change is what will keep us ahead of the world in the productivity race.

The United States continues to lead the world in productivity. We have led this race for many years and will continue to do so. But we must look at more than just the United States. The developing world is quite close to the United States in productivity and has the opportunity to catch up quickly. The technology and techniques are available and can be used by any society able to put socialism, wars, and despotic rulers behind them. When countries can put a form of liberal democracy and capitalism in place, they can rapidly join the developed world and provide a much higher quality of life for their people.

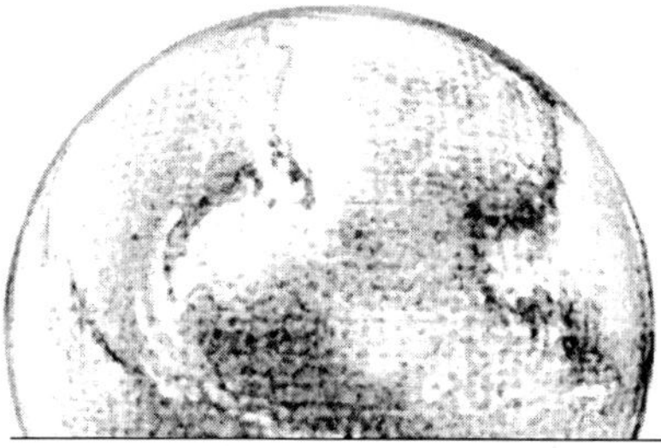

Conclusion

THIS IS A VERY OPTIMISTIC BOOK. In it I have shown that many of our worst fears about our world and our place in it are unfounded. We are fortunate to live in the time period that we do; on balance, things have never been as good as they are now. The doomsayers and people forecasting the end of civilization are simply wrong.

Let's review the eight subjects covered in the book.

- **I: Energy**. The world isn't running out of energy (or, for that matter, of any other natural resource). The actual prices of energy and other resources are decreasing, not increasing.
- **II: Transportation**. People want to use their private cars, and there is no reason why they shouldn't be allowed to. In fact, they should be encouraged to do so. The private car probably has done as much to improve our quality of life in the last century as any other invention.
- **III: Pollution**. The age of pollution is over in the developed world. We are now affluent enough to afford pollution control technologies. However, a mandatory prerequisite for reducing pollution is affluence. Economic development of

emerging countries is essential for the world to solve its pollution problems as a whole.

- **IV: Population**. The fear of increasing population is unfounded. The world, with the creativity of humankind, can easily support its existing and projected population. Again, affluence is a positive factor because population increases tend to slow down with increased affluence.
- **V: Education**. A different way to look at our education system is to look at the continuously increasing percentages of our population that are becoming educated. Over the last half century, we have doubled, and even tripled, the percentages of people finishing high school and college. These increases include females and minorities. We still need to improve the quality of our education system to meet the needs of the information age, but we are continually building a more educated society.
- **VI: Crime**. Contrary to popular belief, crime in America is decreasing, not increasing. However, we still have a major problem with violent crime among our young people, especially minorities.
- **VII: Balance of Payments**. Contrary to popular belief, the U.S.'s negative balance of payments over the last fifteen or so years has been positive for our economy. It has meant that people in other countries have been investing in America.
- **VIII: Productivity**. The United States has always been the most productive country in the world. In the '80s, we improved on that position and are now the clear world leader economically.

All of these subjects have been topics for great concern for the popular press and the general public. Rather than reasons for doom and gloom, they should all be reasons for hope and encouragement. The real story on these topics is one of successful solutions and progress, with things getting better—not worse. The creativity of the human mind is constantly at work and there is no reason to believe that our world situation as measured by the topics in this book won't continue to improve indefinitely.